SHARPEN YOUR BRAND

Self-Improvement Tips from 150+ Memorable Quotes

EBERE ANOSIKE

SHARPEN YOUR BRAND
Self-Improvement Tips From 150+ Memorable Quotes

© 2022 Ebere T. Anosike

All rights reserved. No part of this publication may be reproduced, distributed, or transmitted in any form or by any means, including photocopying, recording, or other electronic or mechanical methods, without the prior written permission of the publisher, except in the case of brief quotations embodied in critical reviews and certain other noncommercial uses permitted by copyright law.

Print ISBN: 978-1-66784-051-2
eBook ISBN: 978-1-66784-052-9

PRESENTATION

Presented to:

Presented by:

Date:

DEDICATION

To Julia, Dave, Lilian, Williams, Victor, Hansley, Njideka, Victory, Endaline, Rosindal, Jane, Blessing, and Elizabeth, for excelling while beating the odds.

To Frank, Pearl, Favor, Princess, Precious, Paula, and Josephine, for demonstrating good level of conviction in their dreams and aspirations so far.

To Steve, Eagle, Victoria, Sophia, Increase, Mercy, Jessica, Damian, Laura, and Natalia, for the promise of accomplishing greater things in the near future.

To **Lois Flire Foundation** (http://www.loisflirefoundation.org.ng/) for its humanitarian outreach program that is touching many lives around the world.

Finally, this book is dedicated to every person that is striving to change his end story, despite the odds facing him. We are joined by a common belief that if a person always tries to excel, the chances are very high that he will achieve a breakthrough and eventually become successful.

ACKNOWLEDGMENT

The author is grateful to:

- Wife, Peace, for sowing the seed about starting a book to collate the daily reflections and support during the writing project.

- Dave, Lilian, Williams, KC and Frank, for their youthful insights into the book project.

- Margaret, a lawyer and publisher, for always being a sounding board, and ensuring that all my endeavors make business and legal sense.

- Dr. Chetachi Oruche, a pharmacist, and mentor, Emeritus Professor C.S. Nwajide, both authors, for their guidance and encouragement.

INTRODUCTION

I routinely interact with many young people within the high school to graduates brackets. During these interactions, I realized that many of them needed mentoring support in their life journeys. Thus, I generally became a sort of mentor. I found myself frequently thinking of how best to motivate them while addressing their inquiries.

It started off with me looking for interesting motivational quotes to reinforce my advice to them on various personal development and improvement needs, considering their environments and circumstances. I researched the internet to find fitting quotes and thereafter sat down to think about what they would mean to me personally assuming I were in their shoes, which was indeed the case many years back.

I would then share the quotes and reflections via WhatsApp status updates on almost daily basis. A few times, I would also share on Facebook, but noticed that many relatives, friends, and associates liked these posts, with some requesting me to forward to them so that they could share with their family members.

When I worked in a training role in the past, I coordinated a pioneer Coaching & Mentoring Scheme for my company in Nigeria and later implemented it in a Skill Management role. So, I have been involved in coaching and mentoring of young recruits and interns for many years.

Naturally, my reflections leaned more toward talent development, goal setting, activity planning, productivity, and personal effectiveness – things an average person needs to do more to be effective at workplace and in life generally. Given my humble background like those of the protégés, I also covered what a person would need to do more to improve chances of becoming successful, despite the prevailing odds, which might include difficult family or personal circumstances. What started as a random update on WhatsApp eventually became a daily preoccupation. In the second half of 2020 and almost entire 2021, I published these reflections virtually on daily basis. The problem with WhatsApp and Facebook status updates is that posts disappear after twenty-four hours. The challenge therefore became how to preserve the reflections and how to make them available to a wider audience beyond my phone and Facebook contacts.

Assembling the memorable quotes entailed a lot of research, but the main work was my personal reflections on them, which were the incremental values added. The reflections have leveraged my personal circumstances, work experience, and feedback from young people.

I often woke up early to compose posts and publish them before daybreak, so that my followers could read them when they wake up in the mornings. One day, my wife asked me, "Since you are doing this stuff every day, staying awake late night, why not write it into a book?" That was how the idea of writing this book was born.

WhatsApp posts have word character length limitations. In course of preparing the reflections, a lot of abridging had to be done, sometimes leading to loss of important perspectives or emphasis. Compiling the reflections into a book format, now with a little latitude, makes them more insightful for readers. Also, there are several concepts or principles featured in the reflections that less mature readers might not be familiar with. I felt a need to explain these in some detail. Thus, the book is outlined in two parts.

Part 1 addresses the various memorable and philosophical quotes, with my reflections on them. These have been organized into themes for enhanced readability and to serve as a study guide.

Part 2 explains some concepts such as Business Acumen, Decision Making, Risk Management, Stakeholder Management, and Social Media in Business. This section is a must-read for younger readers including fresh graduates, while it is optional for more mature readers who can use them for reference purposes. Understanding of these concepts will provide the reader with additional personal development ideas.

Of course, there are many quotations that could benefit from multiple interpretations or perspectives. The reader is encouraged to challenge the opinions of the author, as it is through such thought-provoking challenges that one can internalize the reflections, and hopefully, get inspired by them.

PART 1 - MEMORABLE QUOTES AND REFLECTIONS

The quotations presented in this book have been carefully selected to address self-improvement considerations. They are not, by any means, the only ones that are relevant, but have been chosen to drive home some thoughts and messages for the reader.

As you reflect on the quotes and author's views on them, it is hoped that you will become spurred to come to terms with some behavioral changes you may need to make in your thinking, attitude, relationships, and even ways of working, which will enable you attain some improvement in life, and possibly, achieve breakthrough performance.

LISTING OF QUOTATIONS BY THEMES

	Quotation Header Ref. Nos.	
Themes	From	To
Motivation	1.1.1 -	1.1.15
Vision, Goal Setting and Activity Planning	1.2.1 -	1.2.15
Talent Management	1.3.1 -	1.3.13
Personal Effectiveness	1.4.1 -	1.4.33
Risk Management	1.5.1 -	1.5.12
Decision-Making	1.6.1 -	1.6.7
Focus	1.7.1 -	1.7.7
Time Management	1.8.1 -	1.8.6
Networking and Stakeholder Management	1.9.1 -	1.9.23
Resilience	1.10.1 -	1.10.11
Performance Review and Feedback	1.11.1 -	1.11.13
Personal Development and Growth	1.12.1 -	1.12.13
Success and Failure	1.13.1 -	1.13.11
Entrepreneurship	1.14.1 -	1.14.5
Empowerment and Helping Others	1.15.1 -	1.15.5

1.1 MOTIVATION

1.1.1 "When you feel like giving up, just remember that there are a lot of people you still have to prove wrong." (Unknown)

We may have doubters who do not expect us to be successful. Proving them wrong would really be nice and satisfying. However, what would be a better motivation is to find within ourselves a more positive reason why we want to be successful. For example, excellent academic performance will brighten future job prospects, acquisition of higher skills enables better paying jobs, success at business could generate more wealth, and a new venture could yield extra income to enhance family welfare. A positive motivation will drive your resilience when the going gets tough.

1.1.2 "There is a vitality, a life force, an energy, a quickening that is translated through you into action, and because there is only one of you in all time, this expression is unique. And if you block it, it will never exist through any other medium and will be lost." (Martha Graham)

Try to make your life worth something. Start from where you are, use what you have, do what you can, but try and get started. Let your motivation show when you are interacting with people. Anyone looking to learn from, affiliate or network with, support, or invest in you would be most comfortable if you are seen to be a person of passion. This is because motivated people are most likely to succeed in their endeavors.

1.1.3 "We all have limits. Almost no one reaches theirs. You definitely haven't." (Avni Jain)

You would run faster than a cheetah if a lion were chasing you. You would swim faster than an Olympic Champion if a shark were after you. And you would work harder if the extra pay were mouthwatering, or an extraordinary performance could trigger a promotion at the office.

An average person is often capable of doing much more than what he thinks he can normally do. It depends on whether the person is sufficiently motivated enough to try harder, to excel, or to outperform. If one can find the motivation to go the extra mile, he will most likely exceed his limits, achieve success, and possibly, breakthrough performance.

1.1.4 *"There is no easy way [to get] from the earth to the stars."* **(Lucius Seneca)**

To reach outer space, a spacecraft needs to be fired by a rocket. Likewise, you need to be motivated to achieve your dream, accomplish any difficult but important task, go the extra mile to excel in a venture, etc.

Motivation can be positive (driven by useful benefits when action is taken) or negative (driven by fear, regrets, or possible backlash from inaction). Being motivated is however a choice an individual must make. Find something worthwhile and dig in with passion.

1.1.5 *"You will never always be [able to perpetually stay strongly] motivated [all the time], so you must learn to be disciplined."* **(Denzel Washington)**

Due to ups and downs of life, there will be times when our energy levels and motivation might be at the lowest ebb. At such times, it is our discipline that will carry us through. Self-discipline is therefore a vital attribute of success as it helps us stay focused on goals, avoid distractive habits or temptations, and enables bravery to stick with difficult tasks, allowing us to overcome obstacles and discomfort while pushing to new heights.

1.1.6 *"A man who works with his hands is a laborer; a man who works with his hands and his brain is a craftsman; but a man who works with his hands, brain, and heart is an artist."* *(Louis Nizer)*

Do you pursue your endeavor as a laborer, craftsman, or an artist? Are you contented with whatever happens to you? Do you always need nudging by people, or are you self-motivated? Do you have passion or drive ["heart"] to accomplish set goals? Are you aware that passion is what makes the difference between mundane tasks (chores) and chasing dreams? It is also what drives the entrepreneurial spirit. Try to motivate yourself and become an "artist".

1.1.7 *"People rarely succeed unless they have fun in what they are doing."* *(Dale Carnegie)*

In organizations, passion manifests in willingness of employees to observe the company's core values such as honesty, integrity, and transparency; customer service; continuous improvement and innovation; diversity and inclusiveness, and teamwork. Therefore, resourceful employees use their passion to drive business growth.

It is also this passion that drives performance, the desire to go the extra mile, commitment to self-development and growth, and desire by employees to become the most valuable members of their teams.

If you do not sustain energy at the workplace, you run the risk of eventually becoming a liability, not only to your employers, but also in your personal life. A number of highly experienced people have lost their jobs because of poor motivation, as organizations are often worried about the negative impact of low staff morale on other workers, especially subordinates.

1.1.8 *"Your work is going to fill a large part of your life, and the only way to be truly satisfied is to do what you believe is great* work. *And the only way to do great work is to love what you do. If you haven't found it yet, keep looking. Don't settle. As with all matters of the heart, you'll know when you find it."* (Steve Jobs)

Whether you are working for yourself or for someone else, success comes from tenacity and going the extra mile. These, in turn, are driven by passion, determination, and quest for excellence. Make the desire to be at your best a habit in all endeavors.

1.1.9 *"Take up one idea. Make that one idea your life - think of it, dream of it, live on that idea. Let the brain, muscles, nerves, every part of your body, be full of that idea, and just leave every other idea alone. This is the way to success."* (Swami Vivekananda)

You can do almost anything if you have passion, drive, focus and support. Do you notice that passion is often the first among the listed critical factors for success? The reason is that it fuels everything else. Interestingly, people look out for it before deciding to assist or involve themselves in your plans. For this reason, it is usually one of the important attributes tested during job interviews.

1.1.10 *"Successful people are not [necessarily] gifted; they just work hard, then succeed on purpose."* (G.K. Nielson)

It is not uncommon seeing intelligent and gifted people who become failures, including kids from rich families, who should stand a better chance of success because of their family wealth. Talent is valuable, yes, but it cannot replace the desire to have vision and objectives (creating a "purpose") and then doing the required hard work to achieve success. The starting point, however, is finding a reason why you really want to be successful. It is this reason that will motivate you to endure the expected storm on the harsh road to success. It'll make hard work feel less hard.

1.1.11 *"The higher your energy level, the more efficient your body. The more efficient your body, the better you feel and the more you will use your talent to produce outstanding results." (Tony Robbins)*

1.1.12 *"Passion is energy. Feel the power that comes from focusing on what excites you." (Oprah Winfrey)*

You have a higher chance of success in life if your occupation is linked to your passion. Here are some tips for framing (identifying and developing) your passion: -

- Generate a list of hobby ideas you'll later screen.
- Research the hobbies and determine what skills each requires.
- Assess the possibility of making money from them.
- Use your own capacity, the skills requirement, and potential commerciality as criteria to narrow the list to about three.
- Look for people you admire their attributes and find out what made them successful and engage them to learn from challenges they faced in similar endeavors. Start within your existing network.
- Get peer support for final screening of your options and come up with a draft plan. You can identify a resourceful person that can help you challenge the plan.
- Start your passion on the side to build up skills and income before quitting current job, if any.

1.1.13 *"Nothing great in the world has ever been accomplished without passion." (Georg W.F. Hegel)*

Irrespective of your capability, top performance requires you to have passion and resilience, to create plans underpinned by visionary ideas, common sense, and sound logic, and be able to continuously assess your efforts through feedback and reviews. These are key drivers of success.

1.1.14 *"Don't underestimate the power of your vision to change the world. Whether that world is your office, community, an industry [team] or a [global] movement, you need to have a core belief that what you contribute can fundamentally change the paradigm or way of thinking about problems." (Leroy Hood)*

Wherever you are, no matter your position, things do not just happen by faith alone. The starting point of all achievements is desire followed by determination. You really must want something so badly to make it happen.

1.1.15 *"There may be people that have more talent than you, but there's no excuse for anyone to work harder than you." (Derek Jeter)*

Do not be discouraged by not having as much skill, access to resources, networks, and perhaps even opportunities as other people. Instead, use it as motivation to work harder, to actualize your dreams. A surplus of effort can sometimes overcome a deficit of talent and confidence. If you have a vision, a credible plan, and a habit of always trying to excel, you are sure to find success in your endeavors, sooner or later.

1.2 VISION, GOAL SETTING AND ACTIVITY PLANNING

1.2.1 *"If a man takes no thought about what is distant, he will find sorrow near at hand." (Confucius)*

Success does not happen by chance. One really needs to think and plan to enable success. Planning helps one to: (i) clarify the objectives; (ii) determine what activities are important and need to be executed, their dependencies, logical sequences, and timelines; (iii) assess what resources and efforts (e.g., knowledge, skill, manpower, funding and even time) are required to deliver the activities; (iv) identify the enablers and blockers to the plan; and (v) know the stakeholders who need to be properly managed during plan delivery.

Guess what, the starting point in planning anything is to define a goal. Goal setting requires a vision and understanding of available opportunities in one's environment.

1.2.2 *"In business, I believe that if you focus only on the journey, you'll miss the whole point of the enterprise. There has to be a goal, an end game of some kind; otherwise, you're just spinning your wheels. Yes, the journey is important, but the destination is important, too." (Ivanka Trump)*

Try to avoid embarking on activities without clear objectives, plan, and timelines. Otherwise, you may not be able to properly assess the opportunities and risks you may encounter along the route, or how you are making progress. What on the surface seems to be an opportunity could actually turn out an impediment if you started off with no clear goals.

1.2.3 *"The one who follows the crowd will usually go no further than the crowd. The one who walks alone is likely to find himself in places no one has been before." (Albert Einstein)*

Do you want to be different from what you are now? Do you want to accomplish something beyond your current position? Elevate above your peers by developing yourself, defining higher goals, doing things that make you stand out, going the extra mile, achieving topmost performance on assigned tasks or job, upgrading your networks, etc.

1.2.4 *"The tragedy in life doesn't lie in not reaching your goal. The tragedy lies in having no goal to reach." (Benjamin Mays)*

It won't be a calamity to die with unfulfilled dreams provided you have given your best shots to all the challenges you faced. What would really be disastrous is to not dream at all, not have any credible goals or plans, or to be unwilling to venture forth; but instead, so easily succumb to difficulties or live a life of mediocracy. Mind you, it won't really help if you just give up so easily or blame the gods for your misfortunes and lack of enterprise. Here are the steps you can take to start changing your life:

(a) **Get busy on activities that create value:** Draw up a schedule to fill up each day, with stuff that excites you, such as: important on-the-job tasks; home improvement projects, reading a book; sporting activities; learning of new skills; academic activities; and learning to play a musical instrument. The activities must be things that create some tangible value.

(b) **Go the extra mile:** Do things no one else is willing to do. So long it is beneficial, not very risky, and has some long-term value, check that it is feasible and give it a shot. Become the person everyone goes to if they want something handled that is too hard. In high school, I used to aspire to be the one student others would want to go to if they needed help with Mathematics. My learning goal therefore was not just to be able to pass the exams, but to be so knowledgeable about a subject that I could teach fellow students. That ultimately made me excel.

(c) **Put more energy in self-development:** Determine your strengths and weaknesses and think of what you need to do to address your competence gaps and also make yourself emotionally stronger.

(d) **Make it a habit to read books:** Reading makes you think, helps your imagination, and ultimately, promotes creative thinking. Don't just fixate on novels and love stories. Try to include books in your areas of possible future career interests. If you are yet to make up your mind about your future careers, find books on how to make money and grow wealth. Try and make sure you have a book that you can read during the next long journey or flight.

(e) **Quit addiction to TV, video games, and porn:** This is self-explanatory. In addition, consider ditching friends and associates who are suffering some type of addiction you are trying to avoid or quit from. If you want to stop smoking, it is counter-intuitive to be hanging out with friends who are smokers. Use book reading to help yourself spend less time on the TV screens and "distract" your mind from routine indulgences.

(f) **Always wake up early:** If you can wake up early, it shows that you are in control of your life. To do so, you also need to go to bed early. This is the first evidence of personal discipline you can show. Given that it is not wise to take decisions when one is fatigued (see Quotation No. 1.6.5), rather than take decisions late at night, it is often better to go to bed after a stressful or long day, and wake up early, say, by 4 - 5 a.m. to evaluate what you need to do the next day.

(g) **Stop believing that money is evil:** Lazy people often see money as evil. Money is not the problem. It is how you go about getting it and what you do with it that makes it bad or good. After all, poor people commit as much if not more crimes than the rich. You need money, to take care of yourself, family and be able to give a little bit to humanity. If you don't have money, there are many things you will not be able to do. Sooner or later, you will have very few friends. The issue with money is about whether we throw away our values while chasing it.

(h) **Never surrender on the things you truly want:** Don't give up on your dreams. Oh, you need to first have dreams, not so?

(i) **Be positively excited:** Many people are often bored, upset, annoyed, or even all three put together, perhaps due to their circumstances. If you want to be above average, then force yourself to be ecstatic about life. Try and stop worrying about things that have passed that you cannot really change!

1.2.5 "A goal is a dream with a deadline." (Napoleon Hill)

It isn't enough to just have a dream. To actualize it, you need to translate it into an objective or goal with a credible plan. It's the plan that not only helps determine what resources and support are needed but also enables setting of short-term targets that aid tracking of progress toward the goal. Therefore, take steps to translate your dreams into plans.

1.2.6 *"You can't go back and change the beginning, but you can start where you are and change the ending." (James Sherman)*

Humans don't have power to reverse lives, and time lost cannot be recovered. Instead of dwelling on the past, please reflect on it for learning purposes only. We should embrace the present and plan the future we want ["the ending"]. The starting point for any journey is actually the destination or goal. Do you really know where you are going?

1.2.7 *"Nothing great is created suddenly, any more than a bunch of grapes or a fig. If you tell me that you desire a fig. I answer you that there must be time. Let it first blossom, then bear fruit, then ripen." (Epictetus)*

We often want instant results, but great things take some finite time to mature. We must do our homework and not just rely on sheer luck or miracles. A venture starts with an idea; a sensible plan of action, a clear scope of work, energy, and commitment; regular monitoring of progress; and reflection to improve performance. This is what will make your dream a reality.

1.2.8 *"But I have other virtues, father; ambition - that can be a virtue when it drives us to excel." (Commodus, to Emperor Marcus Aurelius, in the epic movie, The Gladiator)*

Keys to achieving breakthrough are vision (dream), ambition (drive), clear objectives, and a workable plan. Without ambition, you will not achieve much no matter how hard you dream or plan. You also need to be sufficiently motivated to achieve resilience during execution.

1.2.9 *"If you've built castles in the air, your work needn't be lost; that's where they should be. Now put foundations under them." (Henry D. Thoreau)*

A solid base is normally a precursor for success, and such foundation includes your knowledge and skills, vision, ideas and plans, available resources, understanding of issues and risks that can affect your plans, situational awareness of where help is needed, and understanding of when to optimize the plan.

If you do not have a framework or structure to support your dream, try constructing one. Think of ways to improve yourself to make some progress from your current condition or situation. It can be knowledge-acquisition, skills broadening, and networking to improve situational awareness or to access more opportunities. You should also be willing to modify your plan or strategy if what you are presently doing requires serious adjustment.

1.2.10 *"I find that when you have a real interest in life and a curious life, that sleep is not the most important thing." (Martha Stewart)*

If "real interest in life" means passion, and "a curious life" means a bright idea, then "sleep" would mean doubt, discouragement, apathy, procrastination, morbid fear of risk, and genuine distraction from useful goals. There is no reason why you should be found 'sleeping' when you have a bright idea coupled with abundant energy. Please watch out for things that could threaten your entrepreneurial spirit.

Where can one start if he has a bright idea? (i) Reaffirm your motivation by linking the idea to some measurable benefit (termed "value"); (ii) Try and research or investigate the issue more, to improve your knowledge base; (iii) Sketch it by capturing it in a fit-for-purpose proposal; and (iv) Get your most dependable associates to challenge your strategies and plan. That is how you can get started.

1.2.11 *"For the great doesn't happen through impulse alone, but as a succession of little things that are brought together." (Vincent van Gogh)*

1.2.12 *"You were born to win, but to be a winner, you must plan to win, prepare to win, and expect to win." (Zig Ziglar)*

1.2.13 *"If you talk about it, it's a dream. If you envision it, it's possible. If you schedule it, it's real." (Tony Robbins)*

Practical steps must be taken to realize a dream, and structured thinking and planning are required to achieve success in key endeavors. In a project management approach that can easily be adapted in a personal space, the following are the steps required to drive opportunity realization:

(i) Define a vision, benefit, purpose, and objectives.

(ii) Before you go too far, confirm that you have the requisite skills and competencies to achieve the goal. This may reveal whether you need some training or coaching before you can start.

(iii) With your current reality as starting point, determine steps, and activities needed to achieve objectives and timelines.

(iv) Identify resources required and think about how to fund your plan, where help might come from if needed.

(v) Assess issues and risks that may be encountered to enable you know how to mitigate them.

(vi) Translate all the above into a plan to be worked, with some milestone targets.

(vii) Identify people to be involved in delivering the plan e.g., authorizers, workers, financiers, helpers, mentors, clients, and people in charge of the location where applicable.

(viii) Commit and work the plan, and regularly review progress.

(ix) Use review outcomes with stakeholder feedback to know improvement areas and commit to needed adjustments.

1.2.14 "The man who moves a mountain begins by carrying away small stones." (Confucius)

Everyone has his own "mountain" of ambition, dreams, goals, or objectives, whether in life, academics, sports, investments, business, entrepreneurship, etc. There is a popular maxim, "The journey of a thousand miles starts with a single step." To wit, if you want to do something big, start in small steps until you reach your goal.

When translating your dream or vision into a plan, it is useful to include intermediate milestones. For example, if you want to achieve a savings target by a certain date, try to include monthly or quarterly targets that you can use to track progress against your plan.

1.2.15 "A desire presupposes the possibility of action to achieve it; action presupposes a goal which is worth achieving." (Ayn Rand)

To achieve success, you need to have a vision and a planned list of activities to be executed; outline of resources (skills, materials, funding) required to achieve same; understanding of key issues and uncertainties affecting delivery; and knowledge of stakeholders to be impacted by your plan. Are you working a carefully thought-out plan? Even if not sure (say, you are working a casual task), you can still improve through a review and feedback from key stakeholders.

1.3 TALENT MANAGEMENT

1.3.1 "Everybody is a genius. But if you judge a fish by its ability to climb a tree, it will live its whole life believing that it is stupid." (Albert Einstein)

Everyone has a different ability or talent ["genius"]. One must figure out what his strengths are and leverage them for success throughout life. If you just follow the crowd by adapting other people's interest without looking at whether you have the requisite skills [akin to a fish climbing a tree], you might overlook what you are more naturally suited toward doing and will probably never really be good at whatever you fray into. More significantly, you will never feel gratified with your work. You need to discover who you really are and what you are talented in. You can leverage resourceful persons including associates to assist you carry out strength and weakness assessment.

1.3.2 "A bird sitting on a tree is never afraid of the branch breaking, because its trust is not on the branch, but on its own wings. Always believe in yourself." (Charlie Wardle)

There are many situations in life that one has little control over. Yet, a person is often said to be responsible for his own destiny, why? The diligent application of talent (education, skills, and experience) to achieve dreams, objectives, and plans, coupled with the ability to leverage networks and manage risks are the key drivers of success, and thus, destiny.

How is your own trust level and what is your confidence based on? More importantly, are you pushing yourself hard enough with all the knowledge, skills and experience you really have?

1.3.3 "If you don't value your time, neither will others. Stop giving away your time and talents - start charging for it." (Kim Garst)

A person normally indulges in his passion, rightly so. What would be interesting is to find out what talent and passion we have that people would be willing to pay us for. Try generating some ideas. Also, think of what you can do to get more value out of your present occupation or commitments.

Many young graduates are good bloggers and spend a lot of time on social media. Are you aware that there are training programs available that will make you more competent and enable you take up part-time, remote jobs with small businesses?

When trying to review the value you are getting out of your time, please also think carefully about how your relationship with people in your network might be affecting your dream or efforts. Are they helpful or distracting?

1.3.4 *"Time is a sort of river of passing events, and strong is its current; no sooner is a thing brought to sight than it's swept by and another takes its place, and this too will be swept away."* *(Emperor Marcus Aurelius)*

The world of today is very dynamic. Science, engineering, information technology (including social media), business, and every aspect of human challenge keeps evolving. Almost every dimension of our lives is being shaped and reshaped by these changes. Unless you have a plan to regularly update yourself through research, training, skills acquisition, knowledge sharing, and constructive stakeholder feedback, you will become noncompetitive in the near future, in enterprise as well as personal life. Are you geared to cope with the future?

1.3.5 *"Luck is what happens when preparation meets opportunity."* *(Lucius Seneca)*

Opportunity will not be beneficial if it comes when we are not quite ready. Here's how to be ready: (i) Be knowledgeable through focused learning (internet is now a huge library; you'll find almost anything there); (ii) Acquire vocational skills in target areas through training or internship; (iii) Have strong business acumen from basic knowledge of IT, social media, business, and finance; (iv) Be able to draw up a vision and formulate a sensible plan, leveraging people that can help challenge your ideas and also drive you to excel; and (v) Be positively minded, stay alert, and update yourself by learning from networks.

1.3.6 *"No man was ever so completely skilled in the conduct of life, as not to receive new information from age and experience." (Richard Steele)*

Growth requires continuous learning, not only for capacity building, but also to imbibe resilience needed to cope with an ever-changing world. You need to commit to learning something new every week. In this regard, knowledge-sharing supported by quality networks is important.

1.3.7 *"One can't conceive anything so strange and so implausible that it hasn't already been said by one philosopher or another." (René Descartes)*

Few things are new under the sun. So, instead of always trying to reinvent the wheel; it's better to learn from others and improve on their experiences. The key is to identify your knowledge gaps, and know where to get help, including resourceful people that can provide support. It is therefore important to ensure your network is made up of resourceful people.

1.3.8 *"The more that you read, the more things you will know, the more that you learn, the more places you'll go." (Dr. Seuss)*

By all means, make reading a habit. Also, get kids around you tuned in too. There will always be something you can find that is fitting for anyone to read for any age. Reading aids imagination by making the reader reflect as he voyages through the author's time.

Reading thus helps one develop the conceptual skills that allows an individual to better understand complex scenarios and develop creative solutions. Simply put, this is the skill of developing or generating ideas, assessing opportunities, risks and options for decision making and problem-solving.

The great thing about reading is that it offers a bonus of keeping you from being bored when you would otherwise be feeling lonely. As part of your personal commitment going forward, resolve to never leave home for a journey without a book you can read during the trip.

1.3.9 "What's the point of being alive if you don't at least try to do something remarkable." (John Green)

You do not necessarily need to change the world to become "remarkable." Also, being remarkable isn't really about your wealth, or the peak attained. You'll be remarkable if you diligently pursue a purposeful and noble life, handle obligations toward your family and loved ones adequately, uplift people around you, and give back something to your community, society, and environment.

1.3.10 "When you realize there is something you don't understand, then you're generally on the right path to understanding all kinds of things." (Jostein Gaarder)

Learning begins with recognition of knowledge gaps. Once we accept that we have gaps, we will become more motivated to learn. Yet, coming to the point of accepting that we are ignorant of something can be humbling and is rather difficult for many people. Feedback, when obtained from resourceful and well-meaning people and processed properly is helpful for reflecting on one's deficiencies. We should habitually seek constructive feedback for our personal improvement and growth.

1.3.11 *"One of the great liabilities of history is that all too many people fail to remain awake through great periods of social change. Every society has its protectors of status quo and its fraternities of the indifferent who are notorious for sleeping through revolutions. Today, our very survival depends on our ability to stay awake, to adjust to new ideas, to remain vigilant and to face the challenge of change." (Martin L. King Jr)*

1.3.12 *"In times of change, learners inherit the earth; while the learned find themselves beautifully equipped to deal with a world that no longer exists." (Eric Hoffer)*

Besides its erstwhile socio-political context, the first quote strongly applies to our personal lives too. To effectively cope with change, we need to be willing to learn or update ourselves, always continuously assess risks and mitigate them, and be alert to potential opportunities.

Continuous learning is important not only for capacity building but, when coupled with flexibility, also provides a foundation for resilience that is much needed in a very dynamic world. Make a commitment to learn something new every day.

1.3.13 *"Life is like a dogsled [sports] team. If you ain't the lead dog, the scenery never changes." (Robert Benchley)*

If you are not the leader of a team, you may sometimes suffer from tunnel vision, i.e., not being able to fully understand the bigger picture or the challenges that lie ahead. To aspire into a leadership role in an organization or even a team, to be able to run an enterprise, or to excel in an endeavor, you need to develop "helicopter view." You need to have *business acumen*.

Having business acumen is not about working hard but about fair understanding of the "bigger picture". This comprises what matters (in order to set priorities); how they are linked (to understand dependencies and their relative timings); understanding the market or environment (so you know product trends, what matters most to the customers, and what competitors are doing); what affects the bottom-line of your objectives, cost, and efficiency drivers; whom you need to manage to achieve best performance (resources and critical stakeholders); ability to anticipate where things might head to in the near future (forecast) in order to determine what future skills, preparations, etc., needed to stay ahead.

Candidates being interviewed for job positions will often need to demonstrate some helicopter view of a company's core business. You must also have ambition; courage to take risks, change direction or strategy, and tough decisions (e.g., such as quitting unproductive activities, or getting rid of poor-performing personnel); and endurance to go the extra mile when others might easily quit. That's what it takes to be the musher[1] in a team, i.e., to be in front of a pack.

---

[1] ***Musher*** *is the driver or lead dog in the dogsled team, akin to team leader.*

1.4 PERSONAL EFFECTIVENESS

1.4.1 *"Fat, drunk, and stupid is no way to go through life, son." (Dean Wormer)*

Being "fat" (e.g., from poor dieting) portends lack of discipline. Being "drunk" means being intoxicated from illusion, fatigue, or indulgence in harmful habits such as drugs and alcohol. Being "stupid" is akin to wallowing in abject ignorance, disinterest in things that should really matter, or failing to do things at the right time.

To make progress in life, we need to equip ourselves with knowledge and skills to get things done. More importantly, we must also have the courage to get rid of things that weigh us down, and be disciplined, focused, and responsive to new developments around us.

1.4.2 *"The brave man is he who overcomes not only his enemies but his pleasures." (Democritus)*

"Enemies" include competition and harsh environment in which we must thrive, while "pleasures" are desires, which can become weak points if not properly controlled. For a person to be successful, he must have competitive advantage in something and must also be brave to overcome challenges, take on opportunities, be able to limit his desires, and also have resilience.

1.4.3 *"You can't soar like an eagle when you surround yourself with turkeys." (Adam Sandler)*

1.4.4 *"If you want to fly, give up everything that weighs you down." (Buddha)*

Eagles fly, while turkeys are flightless birds. To soar like an eagle means to rise or increase dramatically, as in position, value, or price. To soar, one must:

(a) **Strive to stay healthy:** You can't soar like an eagle if you are unwell. There are no obese eagles dominating the skies. Your health is the most important part of your life, and having energy starts in the physical body. Build a strong body and a strong mind will follow. To improve your health, you must avoid unhealthy habits such as drugs, excessive drinking, and smoking, and avoid being overweight (obesity can potentially cause so many diseases such as diabetes, hypertension, heart disease and stroke). Sickness can wipe out income and thereby eclipse financial dreams and any meaningful progress.

(b) **Jettison the mindset of a turkey:** You must believe in yourself. If you don't believe you can fly, you will never fly. If you don't believe you can soar to the top of your own mountain in life, you'll never want to try and even if you find yourself in the air, you may never reach your peak because of lack of confidence. If your mind is full of negativity and limitations, you will not see opportunities and any possibilities that might be starring in your face. You must shed the burden of pessimism and lack of self-belief if you really want to succeed in life.

(c) **Put your blinkers on:** Racehorses wear blinkers to focus on the race ahead, while eagles can focus on and lock-in on their prey from miles away during hunt. You must focus on your goals and avoid distractions by distancing yourself from things that weaken your ambition and drive. Determine what it would take to get to your goal and then take off to achieve it. To be resilient, you must however maintain situational awareness and have the flexibility to adjust your sail when the need arises.

(d) **Fill your mind and body with only things that will take you closer to your goals:** You must mind the company you keep. It's time to limit interactions with people with bad habits, no ambition, and ne'er-do-wells. Your companions should be mostly "dream-chasers", people that want to soar, excel, or are willing to face the storm and thrive despite difficulties.

(e) **Release those shackles pinning you down:** You must be willing to get out of your comfort zone, set some targets, get new or refresh existing skills, task yourself and take some calculated risks to make progress. It may not be easy to get the shackles off – it might be painful or could leave a scar, but you must act for your situation to really change for the better. Remember, no venture, no gain.

Please commit to changes if you really want to grow. Do not remain imprisoned for your entire life. Take action to change your fate. You were born to fly, to make your own decisions, to walk your own path, to do it on your watch, and to reach your destiny.

You were born to be in control of your life. You need to figure out where you are going (dream or destination), where you are right now (present situation, circumstances, and thus, your take-off point in the journey), the practical steps you need to take, and commit to action toward your vision or goal. Get help or peer support if necessary.

1.4.5 *"A great attitude is not the result of success; success is the result of a great attitude." (Earl Nightingale)*

Do you have the right attitudes toward success? Here are five required attitudes:

(a) **Positiveness:** Without being positively minded, the mind becomes a handicap to our success. We must avoid pessimism and the victim-mentality of blaming the other people, our past, the society, or the gods, and try taking control of our own destinies.

(b) **Self-reliance:** Nobody owes you anything. You may perchance get opportunity or assistance from people, e.g., family, but success still depends largely on what you can do with the opportunities you have.

(c) **Commitment:** A study found that grit [determination which fuels commitment] was a bigger factor in the success of students than IQ and ability.

(d) **Hard work:** In addition to working hard, we need to make conscious effort to avoid unhealthy habits, bad company to reduce waste, and distractions.

(e) **Growth**: Improvement and capacity building requires habitual reflection on performance, using feedback, learning from others, and learning new skills and techniques.

1.4.6 *"Growth requires both obsession and objectivity. The obsession to do things we don't know are going to work. The objectivity to change things when they don't." (Jack Butcher)*

Obsession is fueled by passion and courage. Courage is boldness to take risks, tenacity to overcome difficulties, and desire to get back up when we stumble. Objectivity refers to having a sensible plan, imbibing logic while ignoring distractions and discouragement from cynics with no ambition and being willing to change strategy when things are not going according to original plans. Are you really geared for growth?

1.4.7 *"The only thing standing in the way between you and your goal is the BS [bull shit] story you keep telling yourself as to why you can't achieve it." (Jordan Belfort)*

Blaming family, others, our circumstances, or unseen gods of misfortune won't likely change your fate or anything around you. Instead, focus on what you have and what you can control. Try to acquire knowledge, develop some skills, formulate a vision, define your objectives, prioritize what is important, keep away from people and things that diminish your capacity, and develop resilience to cope with the challenges ahead.

1.4.8 *"We're addicted to our thoughts. We can't change anything if we can't change our thinking." (Santosh Kalwar)*

1.4.9 *"Your thoughts become your destiny." (Lao Tzu)*

- Watch your thoughts, for they become words.
- Watch your words, for they become actions.
- Watch your actions, for they become habits.
- Watch your habits, for they form your character.
- Watch your character, for it becomes your destiny.

What we think, we become. If we can correct our thinking, the rest of pieces of our lives have better chances of falling into the right places.

1.4.10 *"For many outcomes, roughly 80% of consequences come from 20% of causes." (Pareto Principle)*

In his work, "Cours d'économie politique" at the University of Lausanne in 1896, Italian economist Vilfredo Pareto, showed that approximately 80% of the land in Italy was owned by 20% of the population [Wikipedia, 2022, Pareto Principle].

He then carried out surveys on some other countries and found that a similar distribution applied. This concept has found wide application in many areas of life. Here are some examples:

- A 1992 United Nations Development Program Report on the distribution of global income showed that the 20% of the world's population earned 82.7% of the world's income.

- Microsoft noted that by fixing the top 20% of the reported bugs, 80% of the related errors and crashes in given systems were eliminated. In IT software management, the Pareto principle is applied to systems optimization.

- In business, 80% of profits come from 20% of efforts.

- In time management, 80% of useful outcomes emanate from only 20% of all time spent. At work, you spend less than 30% of the whole day doing productive work, while the rest is spent doing stuff, being "busy", doing chores, moving about, looking for or preparing a meal, resting, or sleeping.

- In marketing, 80% of sales often comes from 20% of the clients.

- In wealth management, about 20% is traceable to wealth preservation activities such as savings and investment, while the rest is often 'squandered' on routine daily expenses.

- In occupational health and safety, 20% of the hazards account for 80% of the injuries. By categorizing hazards, safety professionals target those top hazards that are likely to cause the most injuries or accidents.

The way to apply Pareto Principle in personal life is to identify things that contribute the most to your bottom-line and give them the highest priority attention. It could be your studies (for a student), your job, skills, business, and family.

1.4.11 *"The only thing worse than a wolf in sheep's clothing is a sheep in sheep's clothing." (Winston Churchill)*

A sheep is deemed to be meek, docile, or stupid. It is easy for a docile person to be blackmailed or lured into actions he would normally refrain from. Yes, a wolf in sheep's clothing might sound detestable, but at least the wolf has a purpose for donning sheep's attire, perhaps to catch a meal.

Living like a sheep is to live a life controlled or manipulated by others, potentially filled with self-deceit and sadness. Stop being naïve; be smart, purposeful, and discerning if you want to survive in this tough world.

1.4.12 *"If the decisions you make about where you invest your blood, sweat, and tears are not consistent with the person you aspire to be, you'll never become that person." (Clayton M. Christensen)*

If you want to have a chance of reaching your maximum potential, you must be able to link your passion, interests, priorities, preoccupation, skills, time, money, efforts, and even the company you keep, to your ambition or goals.

Do you associate with habits, people, and environments that are detrimental to your dreams, ambition, or career? You need to commit to making the necessary changes, and you can start today.

1.4.13 *"You cannot control what happens to you, but you can control your attitude towards what happens to you, and in that, you will be mastering change rather than allowing it to master you." (Brian Tracy)*

1.4.14 *"If you are going to achieve excellence in big things, you develop the habit in little matters. Excellence is not an exception; it is a prevailing attitude." (Colin Powell)*

Attitude seems to be everything. It fuels motivation, drives where we commit our energy, and thus determine what results we can achieve. We ultimately become a product of our attitude. Discipline however is a must-have attitude if we want to achieve excellence. It isn't just about focusing on goals; it's also about consciously avoiding bad situations (company or environment) that bring out the worst in us, diminish motivation, increase inertia (by aiding procrastination), or provide pleasurable distractions that are potentially addictive.

We should watch out for things that weaken our capabilities and resolve or promote loss of focus when pursing credible goals or even in minor tasks.

1.4.15 "The night is darkest just before the dawn. And I promise you, the dawn is coming." (Harvey Dent, in the movie, 'The Dark Knight')

At the twilight of every potential breakthrough in life, darkness [difficult circumstances, obstacles, distractions, and temptations] may emerge that have the capacity to make us lose focus of our goals or even dim our faith. We must keep our eyes on the ball, focus on the expectation of light (no matter how dim) and not allow darkness to overwhelm our hope in a brighter future (the emerging "dawn").

1.4.16 "There is no traffic jam along the extra mile." (Roger Staubach)

Extra mile means getting back up after stumbling, persevering despite the odds and risks, always putting 110% effort, seeking ways to convert opportunities and some risks into value, working your job or task as if the company or opportunity actually belonged to you, always delivering on commitments and promises, etc.

The extra mile is a lonely stretch used mostly by highly motivated people. Are you one of them, or you are just happy to follow the masses?

1.4.17 *"Character is the result of two things: mental attitude and the way we spend our time." (Elbert Hubbard)*

Attitude fuels motivation, which drives preoccupation (use of ability, energy, and time). To succeed or even survive, we must adopt a positive mindset despite our circumstances. Else, we become mentally handicapped, manifesting in pessimism, drifting, and blaming others instead of taking responsibility for our own destiny.

1.4.18 *"Happiness lies in virtuous activity, and perfect happiness lies in the best activity, which is contemplative." (Aristotle)*

Human activities are done for the purpose of attaining something that is good for us, as we would not usually do anything we think will bring us negative benefits. Happiness, as sole objective of life, is therefore a dream and potentially unrealistic (thus, "contemplative"). It must be linked to activities that we hope will bring us some good. So, rather than just aim to be happy, we need to try doing more of things that will make us happier while creating some positive value for ourselves and the environment.

According to Helen Keller, "Happiness is attained through fidelity to a worthy purpose". You don't find, make, or choose happiness. To be happy, you need to understand who you are, your circumstances or situation, whom you want to be, and engage more in things and activities that bring the most meaning and sustainable contentment to your life, while moderating your desires.

1.4.19 *"Procrastination makes easy things hard, and hard things even harder." (Mason Cooley)*

1.4.20 *"Punctuality is not just limited to arriving at a place at right time, it is also about taking actions at right time."* *(Amit Kalantri)*

Discipline is a habit, not a one-off attribute. You can be on time, say to an occasion, a meeting, or a decision point in a life endeavor, but if you always fail to take important decisions in a timely manner, you will never realize your dream, achieve success (except by sheer luck), or reach your full potential in life.

Procrastination and lateness are some of the famous hallmarks of poorly disciplined and ineffective people, and key reasons why many talented people often fail. Never put off till tomorrow what you can do today.

1.4.21 *"Every successful person in the world is a hustler one way or another. We all hustle to get where we need to be. Only a fool would sit around and wait on another man to feed him."* *(K'wan)*

Hustling means working hard every day, doing things other people are not willing to do, going the extra mile, doing them with a sense of urgency, yet joy and purpose. Hustling is the determination to succeed despite real difficulties. This can almost be considered as one synonym for resilience. Are you resilient?

1.4.22 *"I will not erase all my hard work this week because it's the weekend."* *(Unknown)*

A person that works hard is entitled to good rest, but "it's the weekend" in the above statement can be likened to a person that is normally focused allowing a moment of apathy, recklessness, indiscretion, bad judgement, bad company, avoidable trip, poor safety attitude, or undue security exposure to ruin all he has worked for over time. Be on the lookout for potential threats to your vision, goals, plans, and efforts.

1.4.23 *"There are two types of pain you will go through in life: the pains of discipline and regret. Discipline weighs ounces, while regret weighs tons." (Jim Rohn)*

Discipline is a regimen, activity or exercise that develops or improves a skill. Some shy away from discipline as it entails extra effort. Yet, it's still better to face the consequence of being disciplined, rather than regret from indiscipline that is often prolonged and thus a heavier burden. Examples are health issue that can result from poor dieting habits, and lack of preparation that results in failing a critical or milestone examination.

1.4.24 *"I would venture to guess that the biggest reason creative types don't produce isn't because they don't have vision or talent. In most cases, it's lack of discipline." (Jocko Willink)*

Indiscipline typically manifests in many ways: (i) reluctance to task oneself to address visible necessities; (ii) Non-use of common sense and logic in decision-making; (iii) inability to keep away from people and situations that negatively influence us; (iv) unwillingness to review own actions to identify improvement opportunities; (v) inability to commit to seeking help when needed; (vi) poor risk oversight or unwillingness to assess risks before diving into issues; or (vii) resort to self-denial when in bad situations. Think of what you can do to strengthen yourself.

1.4.25 *"You can have all the talent in the world, but it's the ability to go out there every day and try to get better. That's the key to being successful and being successful for a long time." (Julio Jones)*

Nothing is more common than talented people who are failures. The difference between failure and success isn't always lack of opportunities or resources, but inability to identify and leverage talent, risk aversity and reluctance to take decisions. Decisions are measured by actions taken. Where there's no action, there's no commitment. Stop procrastinating today.

1.4.26 *"Motivation may be what starts you off, but it's habit that keeps you going back for more." (Miya Yamanouchi)*

No matter how strongly motivated you really are, it is habit – good or bad – that determines whether you would be successful or otherwise. The following are examples of good habits: (i) Having a vision and a sensible plan; (ii) Personal discipline; (iii) Tact in handling difficult people and complex situations; (iv) Grit or endurance (people quitting on difficult tasks is very common!); (v) Ability to identify and isolate nuisance and avoid distractions; and (vi) Strong desire to go the extra mile.

Yet, to sustain a good habit, one needs to be disciplined. It is discipline that will sustain you in times when your motivation is somewhat diminished because of certain circumstances.

1.4.27 *"You have power over your mind – not outside events. Realize this, and you will find strength." (Emperor Marcus Aurelius)*

Life is 10% what happens to us and 90% how we react to it. To wit, there are many things outside our control. Once we come to the realization that what really matters most is how we deal with circumstances rather than how we can control them per se, we'll come closer to properly channeling our energies.

1.4.28 *"Bravery means finding something more important than fear." (Michael Hyatt)*

Brave people aren't necessarily fearless; they've simply found something that matters more to them than the fear of failure. Let's say, you want to start a venture, you need to find a reason that has very important meaning to you that will drive your zeal. It could be dream of better income for a more fulfilling life, provision for your family's future, desire to distinguish yourself in an area of specialty, or desire to use proceeds to empower people around you. When you are highly motivated, you'll find the courage to overcome your fears. People would then see you as brave.

1.4.29 *"If you want something you never had, you have to do something you've never done." (Thomas Jefferson)*

According to a quote often attributed to Albeit Einstein, "It is only a mad man that would keep doing the same thing but expect a different result." To wit, if you really want to achieve anything special such as outstanding academic performance, a higher paying job, promotion at workplace, earning more income, or breakthrough performance, you need to do something different.

You need to get out your comfort zone, think outside the box, change attitude or effort, take calculated risks, be willing to go the extra mile, have desire to develop more talent (say, through acquiring new skills or refreshing existing knowledge), manage stakeholders better; and habitually find out what the market now looks or trends like and what your competition is doing. On top of all these, you must avoid pessimism and silo mentality, and be willing to get help if needed.

1.4.30 *"The good news is you don't need to be brilliant to be wise. The bad news is that without wisdom, brilliance isn't enough." (Barry Schwartz)*

Practical wisdom, not intelligence, is what enables other virtues – discipline, honesty, kindness, and courage, to be displayed at the right time and in the right way. Such wisdom is generally within the grasp of everyone who wants to focus on his dreams and obligations.

1.4.31 "The most authentic thing about us is our capacity to create, to overcome, to endure, to transform, to love and to be greater than our suffering." (Ben Okri)

Our capability and tenacity are really the primary human foundations for hope to achieve our aspirations. So, before you can give up, you need to demonstrate to yourself that you have maximized your natural potential or inner strength. This requires you to firstly discover your talent and know your capability. Secondly, you need to make sure you give every challenge the best shot possible.

1.4.32 "It's not the load that breaks you down, it's the way you carry it." (Lou Holtz)

Every solution you see today was once a problem. So, overcoming a problem will make you more resilient and motivate you to achieve greater heights. There are however some options for handling obstacles.

Besides giving up and abandoning the objectives, one can also integrate the problem into the plan and managing it as downside risk or formulate a different approach that does not entail dealing with the specific obstacle. Try to evaluate your options instead of just quitting on your goals.

1.4.33 "An Olympian doesn't obsess over winning a gold medal; they focus on doing the things they need to do to win the gold medal. If they execute according to their plan, the result will be gold." (Steve McKenzie)

Success isn't a destination; it is a journey. The road to success entails a credible goal, diligent work, imbibing excellence, and being resilient. With these, win or lose, we would be contented that we've given our best to the task at hand, and will end up somewhere substantially different from our starting points.

1.5 RISK MANAGEMENT

***1.5.1** "If the highest aim of a captain were to preserve his ship, he would keep it in port forever." (Thomas Aquinas)*

If the lion does not hunt, it will eventually starve to death. If we don't invest, even our savings will ultimately lose value over time due to inflation. Likewise, for us to improve our lives, or even remain competitive in most areas of life, we must venture, i.e., take calculated risks and commit to personal development and improvement efforts. Remember, it is only when we take chances that our lives will improve dramatically.

***1.5.2** "If you'd be a real seeker after truth, it's necessary that at least once in your life you doubt, as far as possible, all things." (René Descartes)*

It's often useful to challenge existing beliefs, opinions, assumptions, or their basis. Also, it is wise to try figuring out, during planning, possible events (uncertainties and risks) that can occur during activity execution to guide their mitigation. *Skepticism* (taking an inference to be false in order to question its validity) is a useful tool for conducting risk assessment and growing knowledge.

***1.5.3** "Life begins at the end of your comfort zone." (Neale Walsh)*

There can't be breakthroughs without risk taking. Risks can be upsides (opportunities) or downsides (threats). Rather than worry about failure risk, we should develop the skill to quickly identify potential opportunities and threats and figure out how to incorporate them into our plans, activities, and decision making. You will become more resilient if you habitually assess risks and think of how to manage them in your endeavors.

1.5.4 *"The bravest are surely those who have the clearest vision of what is before them, glory and danger alike, and yet notwithstanding, go out to meet it." (Thucydides)*

Brave people stand out largely because of their willingness to confront risks, one of the key qualities of entrepreneurs. Effective risk taking however requires one to be knowledgeable, willing to learn, be honest to himself (i.e., have integrity), be tenacious and not fear failure, in addition to usual attributes of ambition, drive and focus. Do you have what it takes to be a successful entrepreneur in a world where opportunities are now more challenging?

1.5.5 *"When written in Chinese, the word 'crisis' consists of two characters; one stands for danger and the other represents opportunity." (John F. Kennedy).*

This quote, though linguistically incorrect, is still famously used in the business world to draw attention to how challenges can become opportunities. Yes, every solution you see today was formulated or designed to address a past problem. Challenges can therefore become stepping-stones to greater heights. So, you should not let the size of the challenge overwhelm you. Instead, try focusing on the size of the prize.

1.5.6 *"There is a tide in the affairs of men, which taken at the flood, leads on to fortune. Omitted, all the voyage of their life is bound in shallows and in miseries. On such a full sea are we now afloat; And we must take the current when it serves, or lose our ventures." (Brutus, in Shakespeare's Julius Caesar)*

Challenges of fate ["tides"] may be hazards or opportunities. If handled in a timely manner and with preparedness ["taken at the flood"], these can lead us to success ["fortunes"]. However, preparedness entails having knowledge, skills, determination, and vigilance to recognize risks and challenges in order to effectively manage them.

Additionally, we must also be willing to take decisive actions ["take the current when it serves"] to really achieve success.

Failure to identify, interpret, leverage, and act on opportunities correctly and in a timely manner can leave one static ["bound in shallows"] or make one a failure [result "in miseries"].

1.5.7 *"Good things come to people who wait, but better things come to those who go out and get them." (Abraham Lincoln)*

1.5.8 *"In any situation, the best thing you can do is the right thing; the next best thing you can do is the wrong thing; the worst thing you can do is nothing." (Theodore Roosevelt)*

Successful people are hustlers one way or another. Hustling is doing hard stuff that other people are less willing to do, going the extra mile, and taking calculated risks. Only hustlers that venture will be able to convert opportunities into value. If you hustle, you will either succeed or become wiser if you fail.

If you don't venture (that means, you decide to do nothing), say, because of fear of failure, you will never be successful. Only those who take calculated risks and are willing to accept possibility of failure will eventually attain success and breakthroughs in ventures.

1.5.9 *"Trust because you are willing to accept the risk, not because it's safe or certain." (Aamir Sarfraz)*

Surviving daily challenges requires us to be able to manage risks effectively. We can do so by accepting or avoiding it. Risk *acceptance* means considering that an uncertain event could happen and thus make adequate provisions to cushion its impact. Conversely, risk *avoidance* means choosing a different strategy that excludes dealing with the risk in question while pursuing a goal. Therefore, risks should not always be feared but managed. Remember, opportunities have been known to arise from being able to effectively handle risks.

1.5.10 *"There's no chance, no destiny, no fate, that can hinder the firm resolve of a determined soul." (Ella Wilcox)*

1.5.11 *"If something is important enough, even if the odds are stacked against you, you should still do it." (Elon Musk)*

Odds or risks can be opportunities or threats, but opportunities are often missed because we fixate too much on the threats. What is required is risk assessment, before diving into any plan. Valuable ideas should only be aborted if there are no effective ways to manage their associated risks. Remember, no venture, no gain.

With doggedness, some challenges can be turned into opportunities. For example, instead of taking a high-interest loan, a start-up business can be financed with smaller amount of capital, if appropriate scaling is applied. Some challenges may be avoided by modifying the strategy, while others may have to be integrated into plans and treated as risks. The ability to overcome challenges is what will make you resilient.

1.5.12 *"It wasn't raining when Noah built the Ark." (Howard Ruff)*

It would have been too late had Noah waited for the storm clouds to subside before starting to build the ark. Also, Egypt prepared for drought aided by Joseph's vision and through upfront planning. You need to avoid indecisiveness and procrastination once decision options are clear.

We need to make provisions for unforeseen disasters, by providing adequate contingencies such as taking insurance for your health, fire, household equipment and automobile assets, personal life, and kids' future higher education.

1.6 DECISION-MAiKING

1.6.1 *"Data is not information, information is not knowledge, knowledge is not understanding, understanding is not wisdom." (Clifford Stoll)*

Data is observed events and facts. *Information* is what we can infer from observed data through scrutiny and analysis. *Understanding* comes from internalizing the meaning of available *knowledge* through feedback and reflections. *Wisdom* comes from applying understanding toward quality *decisions*. We should therefore avoid jumping from mere observations to decisions.

Furthermore, if we receive information from a third party, we may sometimes need to go back and challenge the data (facts and evidence) upon which it is founded, before we start using such information for higher objectives such as forming our own opinions and, ultimately, taking decisions. For example, we must be careful assuming that whatever information is shared on social media is necessarily true; it should be challenged and tested where possible, if you need to use same for critical decisions, or want to re-forward to other people.

To improve our daily lives, we should routinely inject some analyses, thoughts, and wise counsel into whatever we do.

1.6.2 *"Truthiness is the belief or assertion that a particular statement is true based on the intuition or perceptions [gut feelings] of some individuals, without regard to evidence, logic, intellectual examination, or facts." (Stephen Colbert, US Comedian in the satire program, 'The Colbert Report', [Wikipedia, 2022, Truthiness])*

Yes, gut feelings are vital to our survival instincts. However, business decisions are only robust when supported by empirical data, material facts, evidence, and logical reasoning. Are your decisions always based on pure instincts or are they structured and always tries to incorporate all key information?

1.6.3 *"Having lived long, I have experienced many instances of being obliged by better information or fuller consideration to change opinions, even on important subjects, which I once thought right, but found to be otherwise." (Benjamin Franklin)*

We can't assure decisions taken today will remain valid tomorrow, especially considering the dynamic world we live in presently. Nonetheless, we must be pragmatic when taking decisions; else, we'll never make any progress. To enhance decision-making and chances of success in endeavors, we must be open-minded, and routinely imbibe critical thinking, risk assessment and stakeholder feedback.

1.6.4 *"You can't make decisions based on fear and the possibility of what might happen. If you obsess over whether you are making the right decision, you are basically assuming that the universe will reward you for one thing and punish you for another." (Michelle Obama)*

The universe has no fixed agenda. According to Paulo Coelho, "When you want something, all the universe conspires in helping you to achieve it." Everything works toward decisions you take, whether right or wrong.

Good decisions generally lead to good outcomes, and vice versa. Therefore, you need to focus more on always taking quality decisions and doing risk assessment using the best information available.

1.6.5 *"The H.A.L.T. method. Never make a decision when you are hungry, angry, lonely, or tired." (David DeNotaris)*

The following are scenarios when we should refrain from taking decisions that have irreversible consequences:

(a) **When hungry:** Hunger makes one more likely to compromise own values, and settle for small, short-term rewards rather than wait for delayed but larger benefits. This partly contributes to why many small businesses do not grow.

(b) **When angry:** Angry people tend to rely more on instincts and shortcuts than systematic reasoning. Also, they are often quick to blame others, rather than examine themselves and situations properly.

(c) **When lonely:** Loneliness causes perception of less self-control, which often manifests in reluctance to take risks. Yet, risks, when properly evaluated, can carry huge rewards, especially in business and enterprise. Always try to find a support system to challenge your thoughts and plans to improve decision-making, rather than go into risky ventures without seeking valuable third-party inputs. Many people have been duped by entering seemingly mouthwatering ventures and Ponzi schemes, which they hid from their close associates or family members. Getting a support system not only promotes improved decision-making, but also helps one overcome depression or emotional challenges.

(d) **When tired:** Fatigue leads to inability to identify risks properly and robustly, irrational reasoning, incoherent action planning, and unclear strategy to manage stakeholders. Besides fatigue occasioned by physical and mental exhaustion, some medications, narcotics, and excessive alcohol also have similar impacts. You must avoid being impaired prior to, or while at work. For job holders, it is particularly dangerous to suffer hangover effects during working hours[2]. If you are not sober at work, sooner or later, your career will be ruined from lack of mental alertness. Also, try to get rest before taking important or critical decisions that require clear thinking and consideration of all critical information.

1.6.6 *"The most difficult thing is the decision to act, the rest is merely tenacity." (Amelia Earhart)*

1.6.7 *"When making a decision, I've always found it advantageous to consider all the pros and cons." (Sigmund Freud)*

Life is the result of decisions we take on day-to-day basis. For better lives, we must improve our decision-making, which essentially is about selecting the best out of options available. But why do we often find it difficult to take decisions? One reason is that our decisions choices are often limited.

It is easier to decide when we have choices to consider, as one would be able to evaluate the merits and demerits of each option. To improve decision-making, try to generate practical choices or options, understand what they entail, understand their respective consequences, and be able to subject them to reasonable [risk] assessment.

Clarity of choices helps to make plans more robust and credible. Tedious as decision-making framework may seem, it is easier when it becomes a habitual way of thinking.

---

[2] This means, no matter how much you want to enjoy your weekend, you should avoid being intoxicated on Sundays to avoid hangovers on Monday mornings.

1.7 FOCUS

1.7.1 "He who chases two rabbits, catches none." (Confucius)

1.7.2 "Focus on your goal. Don't look in any direction but ahead." (Unknown)

Chasing two rabbits means getting distracted. Distractions could come from your associates, environment, or could result from risky behavior and pastime that lead to addiction or poor health. To succeed in life, you need to be able to identify potential distractions around your objectives and isolate yourself from them. For this reason, racehorses wear blinkers to block their peripheral vision from distractions. Remember, focus is vital to achieving success or realizing a vision.

What distracts you from your important vision, goals, and plans? Are they self-induced (driven by personal habits), or external (driven by third parties such as associates)? If we want to excel, we must find ways to control our numerous potential distractions, as well as people who promote our poor behavior. In some situations, complete avoidance of locations or people may be necessary.

1.7.3 "The secret of change is to focus all your energy, not on fighting the old, but on building the new." (Socrates)

Here's how to focus energy: (i) Create a to-do list and prioritize; (ii) Improve decision making by incorporating risks and uncertainties; (iii) Stay healthy, as sickness ruins all plans; and (iv) Follow your priorities and learn to say no. Multi-tasking may seem pragmatic, but it can also lead to poor quality delivery on constituent tasks unless a person is a strong finisher.

1.7.4 "It isn't the mountains ahead to climb that wear you out, it's the pebbles in your shoe." (Muhammad Ali)

Pebbles in a shoe are daily distractions that promote loss of focus. Examples are poor habits, fears, doubts, conflicts of interest, friction with associates, and bad company. If not eliminated or curtailed, they could hinder progress towards dreams (the mountain that one is climbing) and perhaps wear the climber out.

Yet, if all a person is really doing every day is just fishing out the pebbles and throwing them away, one will also not be so productive and thus cannot reach his potential. Try to stay focused on your vision while steadily chipping away at the nuisance in your life. Some pebbles can be ignored if they have low risk or impact, but those like poor habits and bad company need to be dealt with decisively.

1.7.5 *"Concentration is the secret of strength in politics, war, trade – in short, in all management of human affairs." (Ralph W. Emerson)*

Lack of concentration is caused by indulgence in things that promote haziness of thought, loss of memory, and poor wellbeing (e.g., drugs and alcohol); unwillingness to complete tasks or deliver commitments (procrastination); lack of direction and purpose (lack of vision); over-indulgence in activities that hold little long-term value (lack of foresight and acumen); and wallowing in self-pity. If you want to be successful, you need to identify which of these factors are weakening your resolve or concentration and make efforts to fix them.

1.7.6 *"I don't care how much power, brilliance, or energy you have, if you don't harness it and focus it on a specific target, and hold it there [for a while] you're never going to accomplish as much as your ability warrants." (Zig Ziglar)*

The reason why only a few people achieve their ambition is not lack of resources or energy [capability], but because it is so easy to lose focus and become distracted. You need to identify agents or stimuli of distraction in your personal life and try fixing them.

1.7.7 *"Concentrate all your thoughts upon the work in hand. The sun's rays do not burn until brought to a focus." (Alexander Graham Bell)*

Laser-like focus is a common attribute of most breakthroughs. If we want to excel, we must avoid distractions in personal lives or job. Here are some tips: (i) Turn off smart device notifications and reduce internet/social media use unless when doing research (it would also help to schedule when to spend some chunk of time on social media); (ii) Schedule video games on weekends only, while watching out for its potential risk of addiction; (iii) Jot down next-day tasks before going to bed; and (iv) Avoid becoming a people pleaser; learn to say no on issues that are of little importance.

1.8 TIME MANAGEMENT

1.8.1 "Doing nothing is better than being busy doing nothing." (Lao Tzu)

When you are doing nothing, you at least recognize that nothing is being accomplished. Conversely, when you are busy doing nothing, you are engaged in endeavors that are not adding any value. You are working aimlessly, pursuing nothing credible, losing irreplaceable time, energy, and perhaps money. You don't have time for things that are important. You live in delusion that you are accomplishing something, which isn't really true. It's better to face the reality that you are idle, so you can get up and start chasing tangible goals.

1.8.2 "It is not enough to be busy; so are the ants. The question is – what are we busy about?" (Henry D. Thoreau)

We often must quench many fires of life, but it's worrisome when that seems the only thing we are doing. Perpetual firefighting is not only strenuous and unfulfilling, but often shortens life, as it wears out the firefighter quite rapidly. We need to regularly try setting an agenda or goal to drive a purpose-filled life. This will make our lives more meaningful and give us a sense of fulfillment.

1.8.3 "When you stop chasing the wrong things, you give the right things a chance to catch you." (Lolly Daskal)

Time often seems infinite but in reality, it is limited. Therefore, you need to improve how you manage your time. If you want to excel in life or become successful, you really need to reduce the time you spend doing absolutely nothing, staying undecided even when your decision choices are very clear, being preoccupied with distractions, or being in the company of bad people or those that lack purpose or ambition. This will help uplift the percentage of your time spent creating value.

Example of the right things are improvement of economic worth, health quality and livelihood through legitimate means, positively impacting on loved ones and associates, and contributing to good of the community. Often, we have various habits that negate the above objectives. We must commit to stopping poor habits in order to really improve our fortunes and multiply our blessings.

1.8.4 *"Our greatest fear should not be of failure but of succeeding at things in life that don't really matter." (Francis Chan)*

What percentage of your time is spent creating value? Do you spend much of it on frivolities, video games, excessive indulgence in things that undermine your health, e.g., smoking, excessive drinking, and drug abuse/addition? Or do you, for fear of failure, procrastinate and completely avoid ventures (i.e., by not taking informed risk on potential opportunities that may require intensive efforts)?

Is not better to fail trying, than die with unfulfilled dreams? Whatever you do, remember that it is no use blaming the gods for lack of enterprise.

1.8.5 *"You're already a financial trader. You might not think of it in just this way, but if you work for a living, you're trading your time for money." (Tony Robbins)*

Going by Pareto Principle, only about 20% of our time creates tangible value. The remaining is spent looking moving about, looking for food and preparing a meal, resting and sleeping, playing games or watching TV, chatting with people, or generally "being busy." For some people, up to 90% is potentially squandered.

It would be nice if we could deploy our passion (or some of our less productive time) into value-creating activities. Example, a highly skilled blogger can work from home as a paid social media handler for enterprises desiring to explore online marketing solutions.

1.8.6 *"Stop waiting for the 'right time'. Success is a numbers game: the number of times you take a shot." (Maha L. Karri)*

Don't wait for perfect time to get started on your dreams; the right time is now. A business plan will never be perfect; understand the risks in your plan but get started. Else, you'll later regret not getting started now.

Success is about taking your best shots repeatedly. You will win some and may lose some, but if you take enough shots, over time you'll grow more skill, experience, resilience, and connections to improve chances of success in your future endeavors.

1.9 NETWORKING AND STAKEHOLDER MANAGEMENT

1.9.1 *"If you want light to come into your life, you need to stand where it is shining." (Guy Finley)*

If you want to become successful, you need to start mingling with the stars, and not clouds or darkness. Stars have tasted success and perhaps failure and are more than willing to guide or nudge you to higher ambition. Clouds allow you to drift to wherever the wind blows, and may not challenge you to any specific, loftier goal. Darkness obscures even the faintest light available and hinders pursuance of credible dreams. What type of company do you keep, and which types of people are in your networks?

1.9.2 *"Don't be upset when people reject you. Nice things are often rejected by people who can't afford them." (Unknown)*

Besides envy, you can be rejected for a lot of valid reasons. You may be a poor fit for a job, not be pulling your weight in a role, or bringing much value to a business, interface, or network. Instead of getting angry, a rejection should spur you to become a better person.

Firstly, you need to re-articulate the objectives of your engagement with the other parties, review your expectations, understand stakeholder viewpoints, address any gaps (e.g., in the effectiveness of your communication style), develop more listening skills, seek solutions not requiring help from people (if the rejection was linked to your request for assistance from someone), etc.

By embarking on self-improvements instead of just blaming other people, you can enhance your relationships and potentially turn the rejections into something rather beneficial.

1.9.3 *"If you're the smartest person in the room, you're in the wrong room." (Confucius)*

1.9.4 *"The key [to success] is to keep company only with people who uplift you, whose presence calls forth your best." (Epictetus)*

Your environment consists of a physical location and resources within it, including people in your orbit. Being the smartest person in a room means to be surrounded by people who cannot beneficially challenge your ideas, proposals, and actions. Like an eagle amid turkeys, you cannot grow if encircled by only mediocre performers, or people that always agree to your ideas.

The company you keep determines the qualities of feedback, advice, and support system that you can leverage in pursuance of your dreams. You must therefore choose your companions wisely, looking toward people who can challenge you to bring extra value to your life, engagement, and endeavors.

1.9.5 *"It's undesirable to believe a proposition when there's no ground whatever for supposing it true." (Bertrand Russell)*

People often put out a lot of propositions and hypothesis without factual basis. Many a time, their narrations of events are filtered through individual lens and bias[3]. Sometimes, the information they provide may be deliberate falsehoods designed for deceit. Before accepting people's views, try to understand the facts and evidence underpinning them.

1.9.6 *"I truly believe that everything we do and everyone we meet is put in our path for a purpose. There are no accidents; we're all teachers - if we're willing to pay attention to the lessons we learn, trust our positive instincts and not be afraid to take*

---

[3] *The concept,* **ladder of inference,** *is an expression that describes the thinking process a person automatically goes through, usually without realizing it, to get from mere observations to conclusions or decisions, and action.*

risks or wait for some miracle to come knocking at our door." (Marla Gibbs)

We need to reflect on value of our relationships with other people. Do they: (i) Offer us knowledge-sharing opportunities; (ii) Constructively challenge our ideas and actions; (iii) Provide decision guidance or financial support for our projects or activities; or (iv) Strengthen our resolve against poor habits and weaknesses?

For anyone to be in your network, the person should really be adding some visible value to your life, by contributing in one of the four ways listed above.

1.9.7   *"Any idea, plan, or purpose may be placed in the mind through repetition of thought." (Napoleon Hill)*

1.9.8   *"We begin to see, therefore, the importance of selecting our environment with the greatest of care, because environment is the mental feeding ground out of which the food that goes into our minds is extracted." (Napoleon Hill)*

Whether we admit it or not, our values, thoughts and attitudes are ultimately influenced by our companions and associates. Over time, even our characters may unwittingly become molded by them. We must therefore carefully select only companions that exude the types of attributes (values, thoughts, attitude, and behaviors) that are consistent with our aspirations.

1.9.9   *"The trouble with having an open mind, of course, is that people will insist on coming along and trying to put things in it." (Terry Pratchett)*

Having an open mind is good, especially for receiving feedback. However, we must guard against people coming along and filling it up with all kinds of trash, stupid, or crazy ideas.

You ought to: (i) Have a mechanism to filter out quality advice from the bad ones; (ii) Assess people in your networks to ensure your counsels are outstanding performers or exemplary characters worth emulating; and (iii) Be mindful regarding the type of personal information or material you share with people that can potentially be used to blackmail or ridicule you, and also be wary of what information people are sharing that you actually consume.

1.9.10 *"If each of us hires people who are smaller than we are, we shall become a company of dwarfs. But if each of us hires people who are bigger than we are, we shall become a company of giants." (David Ogilvy)*

For growth, we must avoid people that always agree with us, or settle with only those who are less knowledgeable than we are, Instead, we should also seek companies of those that will challenge us to loftier heights. To enable this, we must be thoughtful, willing to learn, and open to constructive criticism, but most importantly, also discerning.

1.9.11 *"It is the mark of an educated mind to be able to entertain a thought without [necessarily] accepting it." (Aristotle)*

Networks are important, but you will not do well if you always accept other people's views without challenge. Therefore, for your to be effective in a network, you need to have reasonable credentials. You cannot network with people unless you have something useful to contribute to them.

There is a saying, "He who wants equity needs to come to the table with clean hands." You must have knowledge in something, ideas of potential value worth sharing, and be able to objectively evaluate other people's opinion if you really want to exhibit strong networking skills. To be in this position, one needs to have solid knowledge of own expertise area (through education and training), develop some business acumen, and always maintain situational awareness.

You must continuously assess your own knowledge gaps and seek for ways to get help as part of a self-development strategy. If you can develop yourself further, you will be surprised how people would be quite willing to share their experiences with you, as they would see you as a valuable resource.

1.9.12 *"If you can't explain it simply, you don't understand it well enough." (Albert Einstein)*

Evidence of knowledge and effective communication is ability to explain something in simplest terms to a person of average intelligence or sub-competence (i.e., without strong background in the subject matter). It is for this reason that knowledge-sharing practices such as group discussions, debates, presentations, and publications, are considered vital aspects of the learning process.

1.9.13 *"Our doubts are traitors; And make us lose the good we oft might win; By fearing to attempt." (Shakespeare's Measure for Measure)*

Under illusion of doubt, we procrastinate and abstain from making efforts. By not venturing at all, we fail to leverage our strengths and deprive ourselves of possible favorable outcomes.

Yet, doubts often arise from our inability to understand uncertainties and risks, as well as inability to design ways to effectively manage them. We can learn a lot by leveraging experiences of people within our networks. Good quality networks are therefore very important to our growth and success.

1.9.14 *"Even the finest sword plunged into salt water will eventually rust." (Sun Tzu)*

Your environment will always be filled with people. They can be "sword sharpeners" or "battery chargers." These are motivators. They can also be diminishers and ne'er-do-wells who aid rusting, promote apathy and inertia, distract from vision, or nudge toward risky behavior. You need to examine what value each person close to you is really adding to your life.

There are two types of people that should be avoided if you want to progress in life. People with no ambition (those too scared or unwilling to venture) and those who are scared you'll overtake them. Please mind your company.

1.9.15 *"I do not feel obliged to believe that the same God who has endowed us with sense, reason, and intellect has intended us to forego their use." (Galileo Galilei)*

Below is the increasing order of significance of the different cognitive stages:

- **Sense** is the method by which a living thing gathers data about its environment through sight, smell, hearing, taste & touch/feel.

- **Reason** is the capacity to perceive ideas - to deduce & induce inferences from premises and to reach conclusions by a systematic assessment of facts or evidence. *Fact* is truth that can be proven, while *evidence* is information (including facts) that tends to prove or disprove something.

- **Intelligence** is individual's ability to acquire skills and knowledge and apply them.

- **Intellect** is the mental capacity to objectively understand and reason abstract matters.

Your growth and quality of life would be very sluggish or stunted if you are surrounded mostly by people that struggle to apply basic "common sense" in their decision-making and actions. You can either coach these associates appropriately or drop them from your network if they are unwilling to improve.

1.9.16 *"If one does not know to which port one is sailing, no wind is favorable." (Lucius Seneca)*

1.9.17 *"Great minds discuss ideas; average minds discuss events; small minds discuss people." (Eleanor Roosevelt)*

Great minds help with ideas and challenge our vision, objectives, and plan, but you can only successfully navigate to your destination ("port") with average and small minds if we have inner strength to overcome their tales and gossip, which can be likened to "unfavorable winds."

We must be careful regarding their preoccupations of small and average minds that could distract us from meaningful objectives. Always remaining watchful.

1.9.18 *"Shun no toil to make yourself remarkable by some talent or other yet do not devote yourself to one branch exclusively. Strive to get clear notions about all. Give up no science entirely for science is but one." (Lucius Seneca)*

Versatility is key to developing business acumen, growing on the job and in enterprise, and improving decision making. Broadening knowledge beyond an expertise area [especially our academic discipline] is very important for success in business and life. This requires us to be knowledgeable, inquisitive, and to avoid silo mentality by making it a habit to interact with resourceful people to refresh knowledge in many areas of interest.

1.9.19 *"As you navigate through the rest of your life, be open to collaboration. Other people and their ideas are often better than your own. Find a group of people who challenge and inspire* *you, spend a lot of time with them, and it will change your life." (Amy Poehler)*

You will have shortcomings if you operate in a silo. The pool of people around you, viz., family, friends, associates, and even critics, constitute an important support system that can be leveraged for feedback to improve or deliver goals. However, to reach your full potential, do not surround yourself with only people that always agree with your ideas or plans.

1.9.20 "Madness is something rare in individuals – but in groups, parties, peoples, and ages, it is the rule." (Friedrich Nietzsche)

It's increasingly difficult to maintain a handle on reality, or even be sure of what reality is, when so much of what we do have been conditioned by what everyone else is doing, even where it might be wrong. Many people have become drug addicts or criminals from group decisions and activities.

Sad examples of what could go wrong from hanging out with the crowd are mob lynching incidents in countries Pakistan, India, and many African countries such as Nigeria. Beware of your associations and risk of irrational decisions and actions resulting from peer or mob pressures.

1.9.21 "There are no facts, only interpretations." (Friedrich Nietzsche)

It is not as if there is no such thing as truth. However, whenever we make a judgment about something, we subconsciously filter it through our own individual perspectives, which are functions of our upbringing, education, religious faith, moral values, life experience, and even family circumstances, etc. This is termed "Ladder of inference".

When considering other people's opinions, always think about how their views might have been filtered through their personal lenses or circumstances. This may help us glean into their own absurdity, biases, and motives.

1.9.22 *"The biggest mistake is thinking there must be a winner and a loser in every negotiation. To improve your results [with respect to engagement with people] and the durability of any agreement, understand the 'what's-in-it-for-me' philosophy for all parties involved." (Linda Swindling)*

Always try to seek a win-win solution if you want a sustainable mitigation in a conflict or bargaining situation with other people. This habit will indirectly equip you with skill much needed in deal-making, a commercial acumen required in successfully managing ventures.

1.9.23 *"I am not accustomed to saying anything with certainty after only one or two observations." (Andreas Vesalius)*

Skepticism is derived from the Greek word "skeptikos", meaning *inquirer* or *investigator*. Therefore, skepticism is the suspension of judgment until sufficient evidence has been examined.

While not promoting the adoption of skepticism in every situation or as a way of life, it is a valuable tool to protect oneself from believing unsubstantiated claims by accepting things on their face value.

We also need to strive to ensure that information we share with people is accurate and potentially verifiable. Note that many countries around the world have now promulgated laws that criminalize the use of the social media in peddling false or malicious information. In fact, breach of confidentiality/privacy and cyberstalking[4] are included in the offences generally prohibited by many cybercrime laws.

---

[4] *Cyberstalking refers to the use of the internet and other technologies to harass or stalk another person online*

For our wellbeing, we must be mindful of the counsel we keep, and what we share with people, especially on social media. There's a Danish maxim, "A silent man's words are not brought into court." To wit, the ability to bridle the tongue can help keep us from trouble.

1.10 RESILIENCE

1.10.1 "Life is like riding a bicycle. To keep your balance, you must keep moving." (Albert Einstein)

1.10.2 "If you can't fly then run, if you can't run then walk, if you can't walk then crawl, but whatever you do you have to keep moving forward." (Martin L. King Jr)

Gravitational forces tend to pull a body toward the earth. In a philosophical sense, "gravity" includes obstacles, unforeseen challenges, and even our own inertia. If we slow down or stop making efforts, we risk stagnation, instability, and failure. We must therefore keep pushing and persevering to achieve our desired life goals.

Also, because of gravitational pull by various potential stumbling blocks, one would need to aim slightly higher than the desired target he wants to achieve any objective within acceptable performance metrics. For this reason, it is often recommended, when delivering projects or tasks, to set more aggressive targets and tight timelines for team beyond what the stakeholders such as management may be expecting.

1.10.3 "The same boiling water that softens the potato hardens the egg. It's what you're made of, not the circumstances." (Mel Robbins)

We cannot always control situations or people around us, but we can control our reactions to them. A difficulty, if well managed, can make us more resilient, an endurance skill. For example, refusal by people to assist us financially can push us towards cheaper, alternate strategies, solutions, or designs, while a missed trip opportunity could lead to avoidance of a potential security exposure. There have stories of people missing flights that eventually crashed. Therefore, instead of whining about our circumstances, we need to focus more on how to leverage and deploy our talent and opportunities.

1.10.4 "The extra mile is a vast, unpopulated wasteland." (Jeff Haden)

The extra mile is a lonely stretch trodden by few. Going the extra mile manifests in various ways, such as being on time or early to engagements, studying or working extra hard, doing a thorough investigation, carrying out rigorous risk analysis before taking decisions, being more helpful to clients to enhance brand loyalty, being proactive in your teamwork, empowering people around you, assisting others without waiting to be asked for help, thinking ahead of the plans to anticipate potential challenges in order to formulate a mitigation plan, etc.

Whenever you are doing something, think of at least one "extra mile" you can go to try making a real difference. That extra is what would make you stand out above the crowd, and over time, incredibly successful.

1.10.5 "Resilience is when you address uncertainty with flexibility." (Unknown)

So much is often said about resilience, a key success attribute, but what does it really mean? An uncertainty is an event, outside one's control, which has a range of possible outcomes. Being flexible when handling tasks would therefore mean having the capacity to understand the potential consequences of uncertainties (which are termed risks) and figuring out how to manage them. Resilience therefore simply means ability to have a plan to cope with any risks affecting our situations or endeavors. It gives peace of mind and makes our plans more robust.

1.10.6 "If there is no wind, row." (Latin Proverb)

Nothing worthwhile in life comes easy. Sometimes, we get a lucky break (e.g., assistance from others, or chance opportunity in area of endeavor). We must however be ready for days when the enablers ["wind"] might not be available and be able to demonstrate grit or determination to push on ["row"] to still achieve success. That is one proof of resilience.

1.10.7 *"The next time you're faced with something that's unexpected, unwanted and uncertain, consider that it just may be a gift." (Stacey Kramer)*

Challenges such as unwanted experiences and rejections may force you review priorities and consider new strategies, alternate solutions, different risk mitigation measures, project funding solutions, etc. This is not necessarily always a bad thing. If you remain resilient, you may still achieve success.

You should never give up, but embrace emerging challenges, albeit in a tactical manner. The key is to anticipate their likelihood of occurrence of these unwanted experiences by thinking ahead and factoring them into your plan as risks.

1.10.8 *"All progress takes place outside the comfort zone." (Michael John Bobak)*

Every problem may not have a solution, but every solution is a mitigation for what was once a problem. Challenges may therefore be stepping-stones to greater heights. You should therefore not let the size of the challenge overwhelm you. Problem-solving not only gives you an opportunity to prove your worth and character but also can bring you value.

1.10.9 *"Consult not your fears but your hopes and your dreams. Think not about your frustrations, but about your unfulfilled potential. Concern yourself not with what you tried and failed in, but with what it is still possible for you to do." (Pope John Paul XXIII)*

In midst of difficulty, a positive mindset is not always easy, but it can make a very huge difference. Although you cannot control everything, you have freedom and ability to choose your own attitude, to focus on the good but learn from the bad. Enthusiasm can carry you through a lot more than you may think. Set goals, start doing what is possible, but keep working to make yourself a better person.

1.10.10 *"Losers quit when they fail. Winners fail until they succeed."* (Robert Kiyosaki)

Failure risk is a routine part of the success journey. Losers easily quit as they often see their first failure as a calamity. However, winners who take calculated risks often succeed as they are willing to persevere and learn from their mistakes. Enduring, getting back up after hitting the bottom, and going the extra mile, to still get to where you want, is what separates winners from losers.

1.10.11 *"Keep on going; the chances are that you will stumble on something positive, perhaps when you are least expecting it. [But] I never heard of anyone ever stumbling on something while sitting down." (Charles F. Kettering)*

No matter how tough things really are, you should continue to put in your best and remain hopeful, and not despondent. Mother luck will smile only at those who can persevere.

1.11 PERFORMANCE REVIEW AND FEEDBACK

1.11.1 "A man who has committed a mistake and doesn't correct it is committing another mistake." (Confucius)

Mistakes are part of life, especially in ventures, but the learnings from them are equally vital. You must reflect on your performance if you really want to improve. Habitual review and commitment to improvements is key to growth and breakthrough performance.

After any key task, you must ask yourself what went well, what didn't go so well, what did I fail to anticipate, how well did I manage people involved, what would I do differently next time?

Make reflection after completion of a key task a conscious habit, both in individual capacity as well as teams for group activities. To aid the reflections, you can obtain feedback from your key activity stakeholders, such as your sponsors, vendors, or clients.

1.11.2 "There is only one way to avoid criticism: do nothing, say nothing, and be nothing." (Aristotle)

If you always avoid criticisms, you'll never reach your full potential. This is because you'll struggle to correctly assess your effectiveness without habitually integrating external perspectives into your plan. This applies to, not only personal life, but also job and business.

Feedback, even when seemingly harsh, is a resilience tool for winning life's so many battles and achieving breakthroughs. Even if you don't like the person giving you quality feedback, do not throw away the child with the bathwater.

1.11.3 "We should every night call ourselves to an account: what infirmity have we mastered today, what passions opposed, what temptation resisted, and what virtue acquired? Our vices will abate of themselves if they be brought every day to the shrift." (Lucius Seneca)

Reflections help us identify gaps in performance during activity execution. A key element of the review process is feedback from stakeholders, which provides the perception of market/environment (clients, customers, peers, associates, etc.). Do you regularly invite constructive feedback to assess your objectives, plans, activities, and efforts?

1.11.4 *"It is just that we should be grateful, not only to those with whose views we may agree, but also to those who have expressed more superficial views; for these also contributed something, by developing before us the powers of thought."* *(Aristotle)*

Feedback is vital for improvement; this is a key requirement for growth. Yes, quality feedback is quite easy to appreciate ["agree"], but even poor-quality feedback ["superficial views"] can still be valuable in some way. It may reflect poor stakeholder management, or simply, communication gap between us and the reviewer.

Whether good or bad therefore, all feedback should be processed carefully to distill useful messages or information ["developing powers of thought"], which we can then leverage in our performance improvement efforts.

1.11.5 *"Learning does not make one learned: there are those who have knowledge and those who have understanding. The first requires memory and the second philosophy."* *(Alexandre Dumas)*

Learning relies more on memory, while understanding requires cognition, which is the ability to perceive and react; process; and understand, store, and retrieve information; make decisions; and produce appropriate responses, in order to internalize ideas and adapt to other situations.

Reflection ["philosophy"] enables one to identify strategies to apply learning [knowledge] to aid understanding, improve ongoing endeavors, and figure out how to handle future tasks.

Often, reflection is enhanced by constructive engagement with well-meaning people who will provide valuable feedback and other meaningful information. Try to seek out resourceful people who can help challenge your aspirations. Leverage your networks.

1.11.6 *"If you're not in the arena [game] getting your ass kicked, I'm not interested in, or open to your feedback." (Brené Brown)*

Often, we feel that some people do not listen to us or heed our advice. However, you can't teach people what you don't really know. Experience, they say, is the best teacher. For you to be able to guide other people, you need not necessarily be perfect, educated, rich, successful, or famous. You must however be credible.

Being credible means you need to be a person of value, who is diligent, delivers on his obligations, always tries to improve himself, and is bold in tackling challenges. That's how to make yourself credible to give other people feedback.

1.11.7 *"Consult your friend on all things, especially on those which respect yourself. His counsel may then be useful where your own self-love might impair your judgment." (Lucius Seneca)*

We should not operate in silos. Without feedback, our activities could suffer from tunnel vision[5]. Family, friends, associates and even critics constitute a support system that can provide us the feedback required for improvement. However, it does not help us to surround

---

[5] **Tunnel vision** is narrow-mindedness or fixation on a sole objective.

ourselves with only people that always agree with us, or who will never challenge our ideas and plans.

1.11.8 *"Think not those faithful who praise all thy words and actions; but those who kindly reprove thy faults." (Socrates)*

Feedback: (i) points out areas of improvement, enhancing efficiency; (ii) helps achieve alignment and clarity of communication; (iii) facilitates education and learning through new knowledge and avoidance of mistake repetition; and (iv) enables learning of new skills.

People we care about can benefit from constructive feedback, rather than always receiving praises from us. This is because quality feedback can enable identification of improvement opportunities, and risks, hazards, or loss of value to be mitigated. It is indeed a good habit to regularly invite feedback in our daily activities.

1.11.9 *"Strength doesn't come from winning. Your struggles develop your strengths. When you go through hardships and decide not to surrender, that is strength." (Arnold Schwarzenegger)*

Finding strength from challenges is evidence of fortitude. We must learn from failure to avoid similar pitfalls in the future. After each task, we should ask: what went well, what didn't go so well, did we achieve the objectives, did we identify and properly manage all key stakeholders, what shall we do differently in similar future opportunities? Truly, learnings from reviews can help us build up our resilience.

1.11.10 *"Success is a lousy teacher. It seduces smart people into thinking they can't lose." (Bill Gates)*

The justification for performance review is rather obvious in failure cases. Conversely, learnings are often drowned by euphoria of celebrations in success cases. Whether or not we are successful at an endeavor, we should habitually review performance after a task. Was the goal achieved? What didn't go well and why? What would we do differently next time? Reviews are vital to growth.

1.11.11 *"Being a top performer – whether it is in business or on the athletic field – requires grit and tenacity, as well as the continuous desire to become better." (Amy Morin)*

An extra push is often required to cross the finish line when pursuing a goal. This is where tenacity comes in. However, it does not mean being inflexible, i.e., ignoring challenges and new risks that emerge along our path.

To cope with changes in future requirements or environments, we need to habitually review our performance and plans, and adopt different strategies as required to achieve success. Otherwise, we risk becoming moribund. Remember, it's only a mad man that will keep doing what he is doing but expect to get a different result.

1.11.12 *"I think it's very important to have a feedback loop, where you're constantly thinking about what you've done and how you could be doing it better." (Elon Musk)*

The difference between doing something and knowing what we are doing is reflection. Feedback is a key part of the reflection process as it helps us to know what worked, what didn't work, what was missed, who we could have managed better, and whether aspirations were realistic in first instance. Feedback deepens knowledge and is vital to personal improvement. To become better, we should proactively seek feedback from our meaningful associates.

1.11.13 *"A life spent making mistakes is not only more honorable, but more useful than a life spent doing nothing." (George B. Shaw)*

You'll likely make mistakes when you are working anything new. Irrespective of whether you succeed or fail, it is always important to reflect on your performance through self-examination, and, if possible, third-party feedback. Learning from experience and following up on gaps are keys to breakthrough performance and growth.

1.12 PERSONAL DEVELOPMENT AND GROWTH

1.12.1 "If you do not change direction, you may [will] end up where you are going" (Lao Tzu)

There is a maxim, "It is only a mad man that would keep what he is doing and expect to get different results." Also, "If you find yourself in a hole, you need to stop digging." To wit, if you want to achieve improvements in in your situation, look at where you're headed and if it's not where you want to go, stop, and adjust your trajectory.

To be able to change direction, try to honestly analyze your life, come to terms with your situation and set some intentional goals. Try to identify things that are contributing to the unacceptable situation you find yourself in, such as poor performance, poor health, sadness, or misery, bad company, and then commit to changes.

- If you are putting on weight, start dieting.
- If you are getting broke, review your spending habits, and seek higher paying jobs.
- If you don't have any savings, start at next paycheck.
- If you are becoming addicted to something, change your associates that are into same habits. If you need help, be honest and go for counselling.
- If you have a job but are not adequately challenged, don't just sit there playing games on computer or phone, whining at your corner, getting despondent; get up, seek for new tasks, speak with your supervisor.
- If you just lost your job, find a former colleague who would know your strengths and weakness to give you feedback on what you can do differently going forward.

- If you don't have work, develop new or refresh existing skills and review your networks, and consider lower paying job till you get a breakthrough.

You cannot expect your fortunes to improve unless you take specific action to change what you are doing that is presently not working.

1.12.2 *"Even the finest sword plunged into salt water will eventually rust." (Sun Tzu)*

Our biggest enemy is complacency, which often manifests in indecisiveness and apathy toward self-improvement. You could be the best in your league, but if you stop trying to improve or do not unleash your potential in a current role, you'll become derelict sooner or later.

Many talented people so easily lose their jobs because they are not pulling their weights despite their top academic credentials and high potential rating at recruitment. You need to dig into your next objectives or tasks. If you don't have any challenge at your workplace, engage your supervisor. Seek for new challenges that will keep your sword sharpened.

1.12.3 *"Smart people learn from everything and everyone, average people from their experiences, stupid people already have all the answers." (Socrates)*

Smart people don't have all the answers all the time; however, they never miss opportunity to learn from situations or other people, including lesser persons. The average person however would learn through trial and error. This is not necessarily always a bad thing per se, but it can be expensive and very costly if it borders on safety, where seeking a little help could enable one to get it right the first time.

The stupid man has no room to learn, no need for trials and no desire to ask questions, but instead strives to prove himself right all the time and never admits where he's wrong. Which group do you belong to?

1.12.4 *"He who learns but does not think, is lost. He who thinks but does not learn is in great danger." (Confucius)*

If a person does not reflect on his learnings, he would be confused or lost because he cannot apply the learning. Likewise, a person that refuses to learn cannot judge correctly and will constitute a danger to himself and society because of high risk of constant mistakes. Therefore, learning and reflection are integral elements of growth.

Growth is enabled by applying experience ["learning"] and reflection ["thinking"]. This combination enables: (i) Understanding of what works and what didn't, aiding improvement of strategy and delivery efficiency; (ii) Understanding of how an experience can be applied to future endeavors; and (iii) Helps us to identify risks to be managed (opportunities to be realized, or threats to be mitigated).

When combined with stakeholder feedback, reflection is a very powerful tool for performance management.

1.12.5 *"Mankind is made of two kinds of people: wise people who know they're fools, and fools who think they are wise." (Socrates)*

Wise people "knowing they're fools" means recognizing their imperfections, knowledge gaps or ignorance, and therefore being motivated to learn, improve, and grow. Conversely, fools who think themselves as "wise" are generally oblivious of their deficiencies, easily rebuff wise counsel, often close their minds to opposing or constructive views and feedback, and thus shield themselves from knowledge. Which group would you rather belong to?

1.12.6 *"He who knows nothing is closer to the truth than he whose mind is filled with falsehoods and errors." (Thomas Jefferson)*

If you really want to reach your full potential, you must be willing to learn. Learning requires you to be open-minded and look at new information with a healthy, childlike curiosity. Thus, it is better to be ignorant and open-minded than to be self-assured and saturated with falsehood and innuendos.

For those that opt to close their minds to logic and reason, there's an African adage: "No amount of noise would wake up a person who is pretending to be sleeping." You must decide if you really want to learn.

1.12.7 *"Natural ability without education has more often attained to glory and virtue than education without natural ability." (Marcus T. Cicero)*

Maybe, you did not get the educational opportunity you wanted or thought you deserved. Education is important, yes, but passion and determination are key drivers of success. Try seeking ways to maximize your potential, rather than resign to the fate of inadequate schooling.

If going for (further) studies is not feasible for you right now, consider focused skills acquisition, e.g., in areas like IT. If, however, you had the opportunity to be educated, try to make it count by applying knowledge to your endeavors. After all, it entailed huge investment of time and resources.

1.12.8 *"Do what you can, with what you have, where you are." (Theodore Roosevelt)*

To achieve one's potential, one needs to: (i) Assess own strength and weaknesses, to deduce capability and decide what to do about the gaps [through say, training, internship, etc.]; (ii) Understand the resources [time and money] and opportunities available ["what you have"]; and (iii) Carry out situational assessment ["where you are"] to create a sensible and realistic plan.

1.12.9 *"Neither a wise man nor a brave man lies down on the tracks of history to wait for the train of the future to run over him."* *(Dwight Eisenhower)*

1.12.10 *"If everything seems under control, you're not going fast enough."* *(Mario Andretti)*

The world is dynamic. Technology, IT, challenges, opportunities, etc. keep evolving. Unless you regularly update yourself through training, skills acquisition, networking, and constructive feedback, you will become uncompetitive in the near future.

1.12.11 *"A smart man makes a mistake, learns from it, and never makes that mistake again. But a wise man finds a smart man and learns from him how to avoid the mistake altogether."* *(Roy H. Williams)*

This points to key benefits of having coaches and mentors. They can: (i) assist to framing of goals and keep discussions focused on them; (ii) encourage out-of-box thinking, to identify and explore different possibilities; (iii) challenge the identification of risks (threats and opportunities); (iv) ask tough relevant questions, elicit logical responses, and also provide constructive feedback; (v) contribute to your competence assessment, say, to determine your strengths and weaknesses, to enable you determine your development priorities; and (vi) can assist point you to suitable high-network individuals that can be helpful when you need external or other support.

Do you have a coach and/or mentor in your journey? At the workplace, your supervisor can recommend one for you. Otherwise, find suitable support persons within your network. Call someone today.

1.12.12 *"No man ever steps in the same river twice. For it's not the same river and he's not the same man."* *(Heraclitus)*

Water and life within any point in a river are always changing. Likewise, everything in life, including people (because of their changing situations and day-to-day experiences) as well as the society. We must therefore be willing to embrace change to be able to influence it. This requires situational awareness, constant learning, and an open mindset.

1.12.13 *"Don't let what you can't do interfere with what you can do."* *(John Wooden)*

Everyone has his or her own shortcomings, but it is no excuse for failure. You must determine your strengths to effectively use them play the cards life deals for you. To succeed in life, you need to seek opportunities that reasonably match your strengths, always demonstrate full utilization of your potential, while taking steps to mitigate any gaps.

1.13 SUCCESS AND FAILURE

1.13.1 *"Failure isn't the end of the road. It's a big red flag saying to you, 'Wrong way. Turn around'." (Oprah Winfrey)*

Whenever you feel like quitting because of initial set-back or failure, just remember that Coca Cola sold an average of just nine (9) glasses per day in its first year, in 1886, translating to ~2,133 drinks in that year. Today, it is selling more than 1.4 billion drinks per day.

Endurance is important for growth. After each task, try to review your performance (external help could be beneficial sometimes), absorb the learnings, and reshape your strategy.

1.13.2 *"The first step toward success is taken when you refuse to be a captive of the environment in which you find yourself." (Mark Caine)*

1.13.3 *"If you don't like something, change it. If you can't change it, change your attitude." (Maya Angelou)*

There are things we cannot change, which we may consider as immovable barriers, but we have control of our responses to them. Personal circumstances can often seem hopeless, but no matter the gravity, there must be something you can try doing to improve future outcomes.

If we adopt a mindset of wanting to excel all the time, and always looking for opportunities to improve, we will ultimately achieve some success. However, we must not allow our weaknesses join an existing list of external obstacles and make our lives even more difficult. Discipline and mental fortitude are vital.

1.13.4 *"If you are afraid of failure, you don't deserve to be successful." (Charles Barkley)*

Many people think of life only in the context of duality, e.g., right vs. wrong, good vs. evil, light vs. darkness, and success vs. failure. Yet, our concept of duality is philosophically flawed. Darkness is absence, not opposite of light. Likewise, success is not the opposite of failure. When one ventures, it does not necessarily mean that he must either succeed or fail. We should not shy away from making efforts simply because of possibility of failure. This is because only those who are willing to embrace risk of failure have eventually and ultimately persevered to become successful. Only such people will probably achieve anything remarkable. What is important is understanding the risks involved in our proposed ventures so that we can formulate robust mitigation strategy to manage them.

1.13.5 *"Try not to become a person of success, but rather try to become a person of value." (Albert Einstein)*

What is the difference between success and value? Success is often external, while value is internal. When a person is "successful", you tend see the success manifest in self glamour. However, a man of value is a benefactor who uses his talent (capability, resources, network, opportunities, etc.) to improve the lives of people around him. A person of value focuses on advancement of humanity.

There is really nothing wrong with chasing success per se. Success does indeed create value, and the converse is also true. The problem is that many people are so fixated on chasing success that they so easily forget their personal values and who they are once they become successful.

Success does not necessarily need to be achieved at the detriment of value. It can indeed be measured by how much value it creates, maintains, promotes, or nurtures. Thus, if we keep eyes more on values, we'll likely end up becoming not only good people (i.e., being good to ourselves as well as others) but also successful, which is even a better thing.

1.13.6 *"Happiness is [like] a butterfly, which when pursued, is always beyond grasp, but which, if you'll sit down quietly, may alight upon you." (Nathaniel Hawthorne)*

As a sole objective, happiness can be elusive. Provided we are making the best efforts in pursuance of honest and beneficial goals and can produce some decent results, we should end up substantially contented and happy.

1.13.7 *"For me, the intellect is always the guide but not the goal of the performance. Three things have to be coordinated, and not one must stick out. Not too much intellect because it can become scholastic. Not too much heart because it can become schmaltz. Not too much technique else you become a mechanic." (Vladimir Horowitz)*

Knowledge and skills ("intellect") are needed to shape one's vision, gather meaningful and reliable information for decision-making and activity planning. Passion and drive ("heart") are needed for energy and resilience, while a workable strategy ("technique") is required to execute ideas and plans. Success requires a balance of all the key levers, namely, intellect, heart, and passion. Do you have all the above attributes and in reasonable proportions to be geared for success?

1.13.8 *"The key to success is to start before you are ready." (Marie Forleo)*

Preparation is vital to success in almost everything in life. According to the Roman Philosopher Seneca, "Luck is what happens when preparation meets opportunity." The phrase, "to start before being ready" means to prepare ahead of important task, assignment, endeavor, or situation. Below are numerous examples of what types of preparation are required to get to a "state of readiness".

Upfront thinking is vital to proper decision making. A student that wants to excel must study very hard before writing his examinations. Relevant knowledge and skills must be acquired through education and training before seeking a job placement. A person looking for work must prepare a resume before applying for a job, while it is also wise to conduct a mock session before an actual interview. An entrepreneur must develop a clear vision, do his assessment (including perhaps, a feasibility study), and prepare a plan before starting off a venture.

A person attending an important meeting must think through the objectives and agenda before going to the venue. Planning with a checklist is vital for organizing events as well as important trips. Research should be conducted before making investment decisions, and investigation before buying, say, an asset.

Due diligence is needed before embarking on long-term or important decisions such as taking loans, entering partnerships, going to college or university, getting married, or even seeking for divorce. Sustainability assessment should be carried before entering or making long-term commitments, while assessment of affordability and where to go should be done before jetting off on a holiday.

Preparing to be ready may require just asking oneself some basic questions such as, what am I aiming to achieve, how do I want to go about it, do I have the right expertise, what resources or support do I need, how would I measure success? In other scenarios, a more complex evaluation that may benefit from peer or external challenge would be needed. This may require surrounding oneself with the right people, who can nudge, encourage, or challenge one toward personal discipline, focus and improved performance.

Positioning for success ultimately requires good knowledge from education, useful skills from internship and practice, business acumen, defined goals, sensible plans, valuable networks, responsiveness and fair understanding of broader issues and risks surrounding efforts and plans. There is absolutely no mitigation for genuine lack of preparation.

1.13.9 *"Success is not built on success. It's built on failure. It's built on frustration. Sometimes it's built on catastrophe." (Summer Redstone)*

Failure offers opportunities to seek other solutions enabling a person to overcome challenges through avoidance or alteration of strategy. However, a positive mindset is also required because if one believes he can't do something, he probably never will.

Try to learn from failures by revalidating plan assumptions, re-assessing the risks, and tweaking the plans where necessary. Get coaching from people with similar experiences, and refresh or learn new skills where necessary. There is a better chance of good things ultimately happening to people who always try to improve or excel.

1.13.10 *"Success is not final, failure is not fatal: it is the courage to continue that counts" (Winston Churchill)*

Neither success nor failure lasts forever. Nokia that used to lead mobile phone business went out of smartphone market due to inability to update products that once thrived. So, even in the case of success, continuous improvement is still required, to avoid obsolescence.

Likewise, we ought to view failure as an opportunity to overcome adversity through learning and endurance. Even if there is a risk of failure, we should continue to improve as nothing ever remains static.

1.13.11 "The line between failure and success is so fine that we scarcely know when we pass it." (Elbert Hubbard)

Success is enabled by diligence, sustained focus, and endurance. However, it is recommended to use milestones and constructive feedback to track efforts as key enablers for performance improvement. When starting difficult tasks or journeys such as a project, it is equally important to know where you need help and ensure you are networking with reasonable people who can be of help.

1.14 ENTREPRENEURSHIP

1.14.1 *"Nobody talks of entrepreneurship as survival, but that's exactly what it is and what nurtures creative thinking." (Anita Roddick)*

Today, unemployment rates in many parts of the world are at all-time high. As a result, entrepreneurship has slowly turned into a key enabler of employment for many people, especially teeming graduates in developing countries.

Even if you have paid employment, you should still imagine what it could take for you to become a successful entrepreneur. The reason is simple. Guarantee of jobs is no longer there, especially in post COVID-19 era.

What if you were to lose your job? Think smart. What else are you good at? Which of your present passions can make you money? Do you have any skills, business acumen, drive, and courage to take calculated risks? Are you social media savvy? Are you moving with people that can be leveraged for knowledge-sharing or who can point you in the right direction?

1.14.2 *"Even if you're on the right track, you'll get run over if you just sit there." (Will Rogers)*

Being educated makes one knowledgeable, while application of knowledge and experience makes one wise. Yet, if a wise person stops learning, he will become obsolete sooner than later. The reason is simple. The world is dynamic, with fast-paced developments in technology, IT, business, and finance. We must therefore never stop learning if we want to continue adapting to the emerging future.

1.14.3 *"The Internet is the most important single development in the history of human communication since the invention of [telephone] call waiting." (Dave Barry)*

Any enterprise that does not try to leverage the latest innovation techniques and solutions, including the internet and social media will not be competitive in the near future. Are you making efforts to adjust your sail to changing winds?

1.14.4 *"Only buy something that you'd be perfectly happy to hold if the market shuts down for ten years." (Warren Buffett)*

You need to avoid the mistake of purchasing or investing in things that either depreciate, have little, or unsustainable long-term benefits. In an era of market volatility due to high inflation and economic meltdown, talent development (through educational training and skills acquisition) as well as real estate have generally delivered reasonable returns over time.

1.14.5 *"It's not your salary that makes you rich, it's your spending habits." (Charles Jaffe)*

Going by the Pareto's 80/20 Principle not more than 20% of our income will often find its way into savings and investment. The balance of 80% is "squandered" on running expenses, home upkeep, logistics, and day-to-day stuff, which can all be easily justified. We must challenge our expenditure habits if we really want to grow wealthy.

You might argue that you are barely making enough to cope with your upkeep requirements. It may be true, but if you cannot save anything out of a small salary, there is little guarantee you will be able to save when you earn higher income. One reason would be that you have not developed any savings habit at all that you can leverage.

According to Cyril Parkinson's second law, "Expenses will always increase in proportion to income growth" [Wikipedia, 2022, Parkinson's Law]. This means that a person will increase his spending if his income also increases. In other words, one's expenditure is always a function of his disposable income. I have found this to be personally true.

To compound this further, going by the Pareto Principle, you will probably spend about 80% of your salary within the first one week from receiving you pay. This contributes to many people becoming broke far before the end of the month. Many people spend 90% of their salary within less than one week from receiving the paycheck.

Parkinson's Law generally explains the trap that most people fall into - debt, money worries, and financial frustration. The key to imbibing good savings habit is to remove and put away money you want to dedicate toward savings or investment before you start spending on your daily needs and projects. You must cultivate a savings habit no matter how small the income being earned.

One must develop sufficient willpower to resist the urge to spend every income earned if he wishes to grow his wealth. A corollary of Parkinson's Law is that if you allow your expenses to increase at a slower rate than your earnings, and you save or invest the difference, you will become financially independent in your working lifetime.

What is often recommended is to commit at least 50% of any financial windfall (salary increase, bonus or unexpected income, donations from people, etc.), to savings or investment, rather than just spend all of it on increasing or costlier lifestyle. You can defer increasing cost of lifestyle to be able to save and invest more, and later improve your lifestyle using the returns from your investments.

1.15 EMPOWERMENT AND HELPING OTHERS

1.15.1 *"Help young people. Help small guys. Because small guys will be big. Young people will embed the seeds you bury in their minds, and when they grow up, they will change the world." (Jack Ma)*

Helping people not only is good for the beneficiaries but also makes you, the benefactor, happier and healthier. Kindness has been shown to increase self-esteem, empathy, compassion and improve mood. It is also claimed to decrease blood pressure and cortisol, a hormone that impacts stress level. And helping isn't just about giving money all the time; we can give our time, ideas, and energy too.

1.15.2 *"Helping people boost themselves is the best way to make a lasting positive difference in their lives." (Nveen Jain)*

Empowerment generally helps people succeed, but it has two components, i.e., the external and internal (or self). The external is self-explanatory, but self-empowerment means taking control of own health, personal discipline, and understanding the value one brings to his family, community, and society.

It is like doing due self-diligence. It is often the lack of self-empowerment that makes external assistance rendered to us to be ineffective or not achieve the desired results. Have you organized yourself first before seeking external help?

1.15.3 *"Life is a circle of contribution." (Unknown)*
- ✔ *I contribute.*
- ✔ *You contribute.*
- ✔ *We contribute.*

When any party ceases to contribute, the circle will be broken, and leakages will occur. Whatever you are enjoying today is someone else's contribution. Anything you are lacking today is because someone who is supposed to contribute did not. Don't be that person, who because he refuses to contribute, causes leakages to the circle.

Every person on earth is here to contribute to make the world a better place. Contribution is the essence of living:

- You can contribute anything useful.
- You can contribute knowledge, wisdom, love, peace, resource, and finance.
- You can contribute physically, emotionally, spiritually, intellectually, morally, etc.

When you contribute, people will eat, when people contribute you will eat, but don't just be eating without contributing anything. Ask yourself:

- What is my contribution in the place that I am?
- What have I contributed to make progress?
- Am I contributing according to my talent and capacity?
- What is lacking because of my refusal to contribute?
- What is the way forward?

The answers to above questions will explain the scarcity or abundance levels in any place. Your presence is irrelevant if you have nothing to contribute. Contribution is therefore way to go:

- In the home, contribute to the well-being of your family.
- At school, contribute to knowledge sharing.
- At place of employment, contribute to the bottom-line and key performance indicators.
- In your organization, contribute ideas and efforts to realize plans.

- In the marketplace, contribute labor or a product of value.
- In your community, contribute to peace, safety, and development of the neighborhood.
- In the society, contribute to security and good governance.

Everywhere, try and contribute something valuable. There is something you can contribute:

- Instead of complaining, contribute love.
- Instead of destructive criticism, contribute valuable suggestions.
- Instead of being embittered, contribute harmony and alignment.
- Instead of watching things go wrong, contribute ideas on the way forward.

Contribution is the right use of energy. Nobody destroys where he has contributed to build. The world will be worth living if everyone contributes meaningfully.

1.15.4 *"If you want to know how much you'll be missed when you're gone, put your finger in a bucket of water and then remove it. The hole that's left will be how much you are missed."* (Louis L'Amour)

No one is irreplaceable. Instead of becoming depressed by this demoralizing thought, being replaceable should rather be liberating. We may not leave any hole, but we can surely leave marks on people and our community. These marks are what would live on after we are gone. The best possible outcomes for our legacies are to be remembered for our good deeds. We can each start making a difference in someone else's life from today.

1.15.5 "*Greatness lies, not in being strong, but in the right use of strength; and strength is not used rightly when it serves only to carry a man above his fellows for his own solitary glory. He is the greatest whose strength carries up the most hearts by the attraction of his own.*" *(Henry Ward Beecher)*

True greatness isn't about how strong one is, but how one can use his strength, power, or opportunity, to uplift humanity and make this world a better place. How are you manifesting your own strength?

PART 2 - BASIC PRINCIPLES

2.1 RISK MANAGEMENT CONCEPT

2.1.1 Introduction

If you want an endeavor to be completed successfully, you need to proactively think through the issues that could arise during execution, figure out how to manage them, and put some mitigation (controls or plans) in place to manage their impacts. The purpose of risk management is to ensure there are no major surprises that could later arise to affect the delivery of a task. A risk is an uncontrolled event that can positively or negatively impact project or an activity.

A simple example of risk management is how to manage weather uncertainties when driving. To cope with adverse weather conditions that could arise during operation of motor vehicle, they are equipped with wipers, windscreen washers and headlamps.

Risks are often erroneously used with a negative mindset. However, we can have upside risks (called opportunities, with positive impacts, or outcomes) and downside risks (termed threats, with negative outcomes). Both upside and downside risks equally need to be managed properly to maximize value of an endeavor.

People often confuse "issues" with "risks." Risks events are uncertain, but issues are already known as having very high chance of occurrence. If you identify an issue, you need to fix it, but if you identify a risk, you need to have a plan to manage it in case it materializes.

Let us take an example of a road construction project in a built-up neighborhood. Disturbance of commuters is a key issue that can pose safety risks, cause execution delays and cost overruns if not properly managed. The construction activity may create traffic congestion, requiring traffic diversions (detours). There could be properties that might be affected with possible damages and thus compensation to be paid. In developing countries, there may be need to engage local labor in line with project's local content plans. So, issue of resourcing from host community would be an issue, and not matter of risk.

Provisions need to be made for route diversions and traffic control in collaboration with local authorities. Also, cost provision must be made to address host community expectations (including compensations for affected properties) and local content regulations. If you classify these under risk, there is a likelihood of under-estimating the cost and schedule impact on the project. This is one of the reasons why many government projects in developing countries fail, or struggle to achieve their target timelines.

In a struggling economy, higher prices due to inflation are almost certain. You can fairly assume that prices of goods and services will be higher over time. This is an issue, not a risk. Inflation therefore must be factored into budget planning and not just treated as mere contingency.

Whereas key issues must be addressed properly, many risks can be treated under contingency provisions. However, if the risk is poorly understood, the continency provisions may be inadequate or excessive. A higher contingency often correlates to high risk assessment level.

When making personal plans, you need to brainstorm to understand the issues that could affect your plan. Imagine you are a graduate and want to do postgraduate program, securing approval from sponsor or support from family is necessary (this may be akin to obtaining "permits and consents" for a project delivery). It may require just a phone call or a face-to-face meeting. In this case, getting consent from a sponsor is an important issue, not merely a risk.

The first step in risk management is to characterize the risk. This means understand the nature of the uncertain event, what could cause it, possible impacts (could be negative or positive), the likelihood of its occurrence, the severity of its impact on the plans, and what steps could be taken to manage them.

Risk management is a concept that should be routinely internalized to arrive at good quality decisions. In other words, if one routinely incorporates risk management in decision-making, the decisions would generally be of high quality.

Some people view risk management as tedious, but once you make the thought process a habit, you will find out that it is not really very difficult. Often peer support is very helpful for identifying issues and risks in project plans.

For an activity, project, or business start-up to be successful (in terms of cost, quality, and delivery timing), all key risks must be identified and properly mitigated. In a technical project, poor risk management will impact on safety and integrity of asset/facilities and their operations. A project can be delivered at low cost, but then results into high cost of operations, unless ease of maintenance has been adequately factored into the design considerations.

If you want to prepare a meal in an outdoor cooking event or location, you need to assess the likelihood of running out of electricity or gas while cooking. If you bring to attention the risk of cooking gas becoming exhausted, back-up provision would be necessary to avoid delay in delivering the meal. Contingency can be to have kerosine stove as back-up, or a cleaner option of buying an extra gas cylinder and making sure it is filled before you start cooking. This example demonstrates that the purpose of risk management is to identify the uncertain events that can happen and determine the most cost-effective and safer mitigation that can be deployed.

Once a risk has been identified, there are three ways to manage it. You can: (i) accept the risk if the probability of occurrence and impact is low; (ii) put in place a plan to mitigate the impact; or (iii) design the risk out of your solution space by seeking alternate solutions that would not entail that specific risk (this is termed risk avoidance).

In the example about cooking a meal, if you assess that the probability of the gas getting exhausted is low (maybe, because you refilled the gas cylinder very recently), you can accept the risk and not take any action. If the risk is deemed high, you must include remedial activity to address the concern.

If any major risk is to be ignored, justification must be presented to the sponsor of the activity or principal stakeholder, who has overall accountability for the task or job. High impact risks must be shared with them so that they can provide strategic advice on how best to manage. Some risks require additional information or data gathering (e.g., from surveys or research) to improve their understanding to eliminate uncertainty in the design that can cause the scope to be highly uncertain.

An example is when constructing a building. A survey is required to determine soil engineering properties to enable safer design, especially for high-rise buildings. With safer design, a more accurate cost estimate can be made for scope and materials. Ultimately, the data gathering is aimed at finetuning the design. As it would have cost and possible schedule impact, it must be shared with the sponsor or management. This is very important in project delivery.

This risk management concept or principle can also be used for doing audits and reviews. In this case, risks are replaced by findings, which are observations on various aspects of activity being audited. Whereas risks are rated in terms of probability of occurrence and impact, findings are rated in terms of urgency and importance. A risk-like assessment needs to be carried out on the findings from reviews, to enable the auditor make useful recommendations on the project.

2.1.2 Risk Assessment Methodology

When conducting risk assessment, there are fundamental posers that need to be addressed:

- What are the future uncertain events that can occur? In project management, this is usually part of a risk identification exercise.

- What areas or aspects of our planned activity does a specific risk affect? It could be cost, revenue, schedule, production, quality, reputation, or HSE, which will affect future operations of the business.

- What is the severity of impact and probability of occurrence for each risk item? Remember that risks that are rated high-impact and high-probability must be properly addressed.

- Is it possible to modify our activity to avoid the high-impact risks? For threats, risk avoidance means finding a different solution or strategy that does not entail the specific risks.

- If a risk cannot be avoided, it needs to be carried into the activity plan and managed. In this case, what measures can we put in place to reduce the impact on our project or take advantage of an upside risk?

- What costs are associated with the mitigation measures and what timelines and resources are required to competently deal with them. Are there more effective options available? Will management support the funding requirement?

- To manage some risks, some stakeholders may need to be involved, either internally (within the team) or externally. Who needs to know, to approve action, provide funding support, help to execute a specific task, and when are these required? If the recommended risk management measure requires capability that does not exist within the current team, can the team get external help to overcome the challenge?

Imagine that a close friend promises you a car to use for your wedding. Now, the vehicle is not yours. An unforeseeable event can arise that undermines the ability of your friend to fulfill his promise of making the vehicle available to you. It can be vehicle breakdown, vehicle not coming off from an earlier assignment in good time, being involved in an accident, being stolen, or access to where it is parked suddenly becoming unavailable on the last minute.

There is thus a risk that the vehicle may not be available when it is required due to undesirable emergencies. You can design this risk out of your wedding plan by jettisoning the arrangement and sourcing another vehicle elsewhere (this would be risk avoidance), or you can go ahead with the plan but implement the following as additional mitigation measures:

(i) Make a second arrangement as a backup plan.

(ii) If the risk is related to vehicle breakdown, undertake, or ensure that the vehicle is serviced ahead of the schedule.

(iii) Take delivery a day before the event, if you are concerned that access to the vehicle could become an issue on the last minute.

(iv) You can go and hire a suitable vehicle from a car shop.

The main challenge in realizing your vision is to evaluate these options to select the most cost effective and convenient solution. Equally important, there will be a resulting stakeholder management required to follow-up on any chosen option:

- In option (i), you need to consult other people to find another suitable vehicle.
- In option (ii), you need to check the service record of the vehicle and possibly take it out for servicing to assure the vehicle is in good working condition.
- For option (iii), the benefactor needs to be contacted to secure release of the vehicle twenty-four hours ahead of schedule.
- Option (iv) likely requires some out-of-pocket expense.

You can see from the above example that risk, if not well managed could affect business objectives. Risk mitigation may entail extra efforts and costs, while a few stakeholders (some of whom may be external) may need to be involved. Without proper risk management (which starts with understanding the nature of the risk), it is not easy to assure a smooth-sail wedding event delivery, vis-à-vis logistics arrangements.

2.1.3 Conclusion

It is recommended to make risk assessment a habitual way of thinking. Proper risk assessment is required before diving into plans, especially, where significant cost, safety exposure, and stringent deadline need to be met. Risks can however be downside risks (threats) or upside risks (opportunities), and sometimes, we fixate so much on threats that we even miss the opportunities. Good ideas should only be aborted if there are no effective ways to manage their risks.

2.2 DECISION-MAKING

2.2.1 Introduction

Without formal training, we often take appropriate actions in many situations, without much thought, by acting based on instinct and knowledge. However, it is much more difficult to arrive at a robust decision when an issue is complex, uncertain, comprises options that offer conflicting values, or are highly risky.

A decision is a choice between two or more alternatives that involve an irrevocable allocation of resources, which can be time, money, or effort. If we abort the course of action decided, only a part of the resource committed can likely be recovered. It is because of the likelihood of partially or fully losing resources already committed to course of action that makes quality decision making important.

Suppose a man decides to buy a car gift for his wife. He goes to a dealership and pays for a car and has it registered. If he later realizes that she does not quite like the vehicle, or that it does not address her specific needs, he may want to go back to dealership to return the purchase. However, the dealer may well say, "I see, you want to resell us a used car that is in excellent condition. Here is our price offer." The offer would typically be less than the amount paid for the brand-new car. The difference is the depreciation because of prior ownership/usage. The man will lose some money if he insists on returning the vehicle.

If decisions you need to take have resource implications, it is important to have a structured approach to arriving at position. What was poorly handled in the above example was the assessment of wife's transportation needs or preferences, which would have been clarified through stakeholder engagement (refer to Introduction), before buying the vehicle.

A stakeholder is one who is impacted by a decision or activity. In personal decisions, stakeholders may be family members and close associates. In business, stakeholders would be shareholders, partners, suppliers, employees, clients, and even the facility manager/owner where you are doing business from.

You can see from this list that stakeholder interests and influences vary. Some must be carefully managed to deliver the objectives, while some may just need to be only informed.

Many people are spontaneous when it comes to decision-making, forgetting that there is a structure to achieve quality decision-making. If you always take hasty decisions, you will often later find out that some vital considerations were missed that could perhaps have led to different outcomes.

Examples of challenges we often face after taking hasty decisions include how to manage people impacted by the choice we have made, the dropping of seemingly riskier options that otherwise have significant potential benefits if well-managed, erosion of business value due to inability to articulate all key issues and risks that ought to be managed in executing selected decisions, and, in rare situations, apparent disconnect between the decision choices made and the original problem or its triggers.

Granted that many decisions from quick (i.e., by instinct) to the conscious, it is still important to understand how to improve decision quality to reduce waste of valuable resources.

2.2.2 Decision Framework

Consider the process of flying an airplane. When the weather is clear, we do not need to rely on all available instruments. However, when the weather is cloudy, we need to rely on the instruments. Likewise, when decisions are simple, we can make decisions using our own judgment, but when a decision is complex, our judgment may fail, and we need to rely on rules of guidance to identify the best course of action. In decision-making, the rules are termed decision hierarchy.

Decision hierarchy can range from quick (using common sense and rules of thumb), like in small everyday matters or frequent decisions (such as what to eat during breakfast), through conscious (using a checklist, like where to spend your holiday), to rigorous (requiring application of a formal process). Situations requiring more rigorous analysis include when matter is of great importance, is difficult, or involves many people, such as when starting a venture.

Good decisions will not always guarantee good outcomes, and the converse is somewhat also true. However, if the issue is complex, or surrounded by many uncertainties, or stakeholders, you need to work to take good decisions to improve chances of good outcomes.

To understand this better, consider what can happen if you drink and drive. If you are drunk and decide to drive home, you might still get home safely, just as you can also perhaps get involved in an accident. The fact that you are sober, however, does not guarantee you won't have an accident driving home.

There is however no doubt that avoiding being drunk improves your chances of not having an accident. So, by subjecting difficult decisions to a rigorous analysis, we improve our chances of better outcomes. What is important is to make good decision-making a habit.

2.2.3 Key Components of Decision Process

The key elements of a decision making are described below:

(1) Decision frame refers to the circumstances warranting the decision to be taken, including its triggers. Without a clear frame, you may end up with a choice that does not quite address the original problem. The reason is that what we see often as problems may really be manifestations of problems rather than their root causes themselves. It is important to always reflect on the root cause. If you have fever, it is probably due to infection. So, merely taking Paracetamol or Tylenol will only moderate the fever, but not solve the problem. You may need to conduct a laboratory test to figure out what is wrong. You need to ask questions like:

- Is the issue or purpose of decision very clear, what is the problem? Why do we need to take the decision?
- What will happen if I do not take a decision (a "do-nothing scenario")? Will there be any negative consequence or loss of opportunity in this case?
- Are there other things or issues linked to the same problem?
- Is what I am looking at really the root cause or the effect?
- Are the impacts, risks and assumptions well understood?

(2) Identify **practical alternatives** available to you:

- What practical choices are available?
- Are the choices different from each other in any significant way and do they cover the full range of possibilities?

You need to think outside the box. You can even get someone else to help challenge your thoughts.

(3) Gather **meaningful and reliable information** to properly evaluate your options before you dive into one of them. You may need to research the issues or inquire from people who might have gone through similar experience.

(4) Employ **logical reasoning** to select which one to go forward with. Your choice needs to make common sense. You need to be able to demonstrate that the one you are selecting is the best overall in terms

of do-ability, managing threats and opportunities, and relevance to the triggers of the original problem.

(5) Understand the **value to be traded-off** by dropping some options. This is about understanding the regrets for the options dropped. Sometimes, you may be able to find a way to work some of the regrets back into your basket of opportunities.

(6) Draw up a simple **action plan** that will be used to execute the decision to achieve the desired results. Try to think of what necessary steps once a choice is made. Think about who needs to act, how much control you have if you are not the action party, what resources you will have to commit. Remember, decision manifests in actions taken.

(7) Identify which **stakeholders** you need to manage. Stakeholders are entities impacted by an activity, e.g., financiers, manpower, people you need to borrow their facilities including accommodation, people that even need to approve your plan, your employer if you need time during working hours, and those that may hinder or obstruct your efforts (potential blockers). For each stakeholder, you need to think about how they be impacted by your decision, the nature of their interests (whether they would be supportive or obstructive) and, ultimately, how best to manage them.

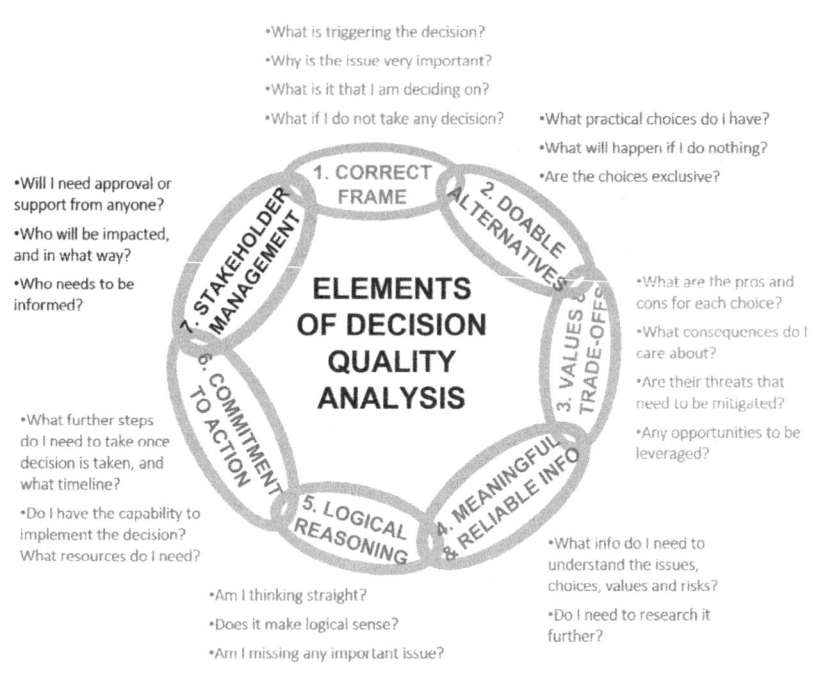

Figure 1: Decision Quality Loop

Elements of Decision Quality Analysis:

1. **CORRECT FRAME**
   - What is triggering the decision?
   - Why is the issue very important?
   - What is it that I am deciding on?
   - What if I do not take any decision?

2. **DOABLE ALTERNATIVES**
   - What practical choices do I have?
   - What will happen if I do nothing?
   - Are the choices exclusive?

3. **VALUES & TRADE-OFFS**
   - What are the pros and cons for each choice?
   - What consequences do I care about?
   - Are their threats that need to be mitigated?
   - Any opportunities to be leveraged?

4. **MEANINGFUL & RELIABLE INFO**
   - What info do I need to understand the issues, choices, values and risks?
   - Do I need to research it further?

5. **LOGICAL REASONING**
   - Am I thinking straight?
   - Does it make logical sense?
   - Am I missing any important issue?

6. **COMMITMENT TO ACTION**
   - What further steps do I need to take once decision is taken, and what timeline?
   - Do I have the capability to implement the decision? What resources do I need?

7. **STAKEHOLDER MANAGEMENT**
   - Will I need approval or support from anyone?
   - Who will be impacted, and in what way?
   - Who needs to be informed?

2.2.4 Conclusion

The seven elements of decision quality are shown above. The idea here is that the chain is only as strong as its weakest link. To achieve quality decision, you need to seek ways to strengthen the weakest link.

The simplest way to use this framework is to think through each step and use them as guide to challenge your thought process, in other to improve decision making.

2.3 ENTREPRENEURSHIP

2.3.1 *Introduction*

The word entrepreneur is derived from the French verb "*entreprendre*", which means **to undertake**. Entrepreneurship is the art of recognizing a business opportunity, mobilizing resources, and persisting to exploit that opportunity. It is the ability to seek investment opportunities and establish a business/venture based on identified opportunities.

Economic scholars have their perspectives regarding the role and function of the entrepreneurs in economic activity, but majority agree that creation of wealth is not a function of land, labor, and capital alone. Whereas these factors of productivity are important and recognized, the "undertaking" aspect, which is essentially the management and organization of available resources to generate wealth or income, is the key driver.

An entrepreneur is essentially a person who owns or controls a small-scale business through which income is gained. The entrepreneur takes risks, is focused, and energized by an inner drive. Developing a new venture or applying a new approach to an old business is the forte of most entrepreneurs, with focus on delivering to the market a product or service leveraging new ways, processes, and techniques. The scaling of the business is determined by factors such as number of persons employed, value of assets, turnover, and/or output, etc.

2.3.2 *Benefit of Entrepreneurship*

Small-scale enterprises serve as good agent for disposal of products and services and have also contributed immensely to the production of raw materials in the form of semi-processed goods for use by bigger industries. It provides employment and income generation thereby contributing to the national economy, fosters innovation, provides incubation of potential ideas for large industries, and serves as springboard for industrialization, technological, and export development. It also contributes to the mobilization of domestic savings and utilization of local resources. It can serve as a base for the development of appropriate technology and provides a veritable ground for skilled, semi-skilled, and unskilled workers.

Technology-based startups are increasingly pushing the frontiers of e-commerce including social enterprise sectors driving social causes.

2.3.3 Entrepreneurs Skills

Business acumen, the understanding of the fundamentals of how a business makes money and the drivers of profitability.

Personal skills of passion, courage, and integrity will drive your ability and persistence to further nurture or re-condition environment to achieve personal or business goals. Most entrepreneurs must be courageous to take risks and overcome significant odds to successfully develop their ideas (opportunities) and make them generate profit.

Communication, marketing, and negotiation skills are needed to understand customers' expectations, explore the market, and source financing.

Leadership skills become more critical where there is an intention to grow a business, which will entail resourcing and managing employees to achieve business goals.

Computer skills: A business will not be able to survive in the future if the entrepreneur is not computer literate. The most basic forms of computer literacy are ability to surf the internet and use communication tools such as emails. Additionally, social media has brought a revolution into the business sphere, by offering advertising opportunities for products and services. During the COVID-19 lockdown, entrepreneurs relied substantially on online marketing to be able to drive their products to the market.

Of all the entrepreneurship skills outlined above, one that is far less understood is business acumen. This is explained in the next chapter.

2.3.4 Factors to Consider for Business for Start-up

In selecting an endeavor to engage in, you should consider the following factors:

- There must be demand for the products or services.
- Passion to drive engagement in activity.
- Capability in the field or area of interest, which may require some training or internship.
- Availability and proximity to raw materials is vital to reducing operating costs.
- Funding requirements may drive a business into loans, which reduces profitability.

2.3.5 Linking Passion to Entrepreneurship

You have a higher chance of success in life if you are engaged in something you love to do. The challenge therefore is how to define a business interest that is linked to your passion.

Here are some tips for framing (identifying and developing) your passion:

- Brainstorm to generate a list of hobby ideas, which you will later subject to screening.
- Research your hobbies and determine: (i) the possibility of making money from them, and (ii) what skills they each

require. You will later use the profit-making potential and relevance of your existing skills background as some of the screening criteria to narrow your choices of what to do. If you do not have the requisite skills, you can consider doing an internship in one of the promising areas.

- Look for people you admire their personal and business attributes, to learn what made them succeed and how they handled difficulties in their businesses.

- If you are employed, consider whether you can start your passion on the side to build up skills and stabilize your business income before quitting current job.

- Interview some people already in the business area of interest and conduct more focused research to understand the enablers for success and things you need to watch out for.

- Get peer support for final screening of your interests against market realities and generate a draft plan. You can assemble a peer support group to carry out comprehensive review/assessment of your plan, from your visions and objectives, action plan and stakeholder assessment.

2.4 BUSINESS ACUMEN

2.4.1 Introduction

Business acumen is an in-depth understanding of how a business works, how it makes money, and how strategies and decisions impact operational, financial, and sales results. Oxford Dictionary defines acumen as the ability to make good judgment and quick decisions. It therefore addresses the requirement to quickly understand and deal with a situation in a manner that is likely to lead to a favorable outcome.

Business acumen, also known as business savviness, business sense, and business understanding, is essentially the understanding of fundamentals of how a business activity makes money and what affects its bottom-line, which is profitability.

An example of demonstration of business acumen was made by Steve Jobs, the late founder of Apple. Virtually, most of the functionalities provided by the iPad were already available to consumers through other devices prior to development of the iPad device. What Steve Jobs did was to bring the applications into a single device, creating a unique combination of functionality, convenience, and accessibility that offered compelling value to customers, suppliers, and investors. The foresight and insight that leads to such creative merging of stakeholder interests is the essence of business acumen.

2.4.2 Importance of Business Acumen

People with business acumen are thought to have high business sense. They can obtain essential information about a situation, quickly analyze same to understand the potential impacts, recognize the options available for a solution, select an appropriate course of action without losing sight of the key objectives, and set in motion an implementation plan to get the job done.

When entrepreneurs discover that changes are required to adapt to unforeseen circumstances, they need to make the necessary adjustments and keep the activity moving forward. Entrepreneurs that have strong business acumen can quickly adopt a framework or process that enables them to think wide to ensure completeness and integration as they assess a business situation.

They routinely think outside the box. They link the objectives of key stakeholders, the competitive strategies required for success, the people and activities needed to produce and sell products and services, and the business processes that support their ability to deal with the complexity. This thinking process can generally be applied to all types of business activities. The framework is often referred to as the business model.

Business acumen also requires a way of thinking that ensures focus on what is most important (critical cost factors), an appreciation of the future consequences of actions taken today, and the recognition that future activities require constant monitoring and adjustment when things don't go according to plan. These three ideas are correspondingly encapsulated in the terms: *mindfulness, sense-making,* and *resilience.*

2.4.3 Business Acumen Dimensions and Skill Requirement

Business acumen has four broad dimensions.

(a) Knowledge of core business activity: In-depth knowledge of a core activity or task enables one to understand the related challenges and thus be able to identify and explore improvement opportunities that need to be addressed to improve the bottom-line. It entails the following skills:

- Understanding of vision and linkage to business goals and activities.

- Understanding of how a business makes money (cost and revenue drivers).
- How shareholder value is delivered.
- Business administration, to drive activity integration and controls.

(b) Financial knowledge: Understanding of basic finance is required to evaluate business profitability, and to understand what drives the cashflow and profit. Without knowledge of finance, some entrepreneurs have ended up with bad loans or mouth-watering Ponzi schemes that promise huge unrealistic returns, which are bogey investments without any underpinning business fundamentals. Financial knowledge requires:

- Basic knowledge of finance terminology, obtained from education.
- Analytical skills to performance financial calculations.
- Business funding basics and financial controls.

(c) Market orientation means understanding the *target market*, what competition is doing and the *value chain* of enterprise.

- Use of IT tools including telephony, emails, internet, and social media, for online research and marketing of products.
- Marketing skills to grow customer base and maintain brand loyalty.
- Communication and networking skills

(d) Strategic perspective is about understanding the interrelationship between objectives and activities (tasks), decisions and costs/revenue factors, market uncertainties, market trends and capability requirement.

- Ability to manage key issues and risks associated with activities.
- Stakeholder[6] management skills.
- Networking skills.
- Decision-making skills.
- Competitive intelligence gathering.

2.4.4 Target Market and Value Chain

Target market is defined as a specific group of customers at which an entrepreneur aims his products and services. These are the customers who are most likely to buy the product. The target market could be defined by demographics of age, gender, income level, literacy, geographic location, etc. This helps you determine what type of products and services are required and how much prospective customers would be willing to pay for them.

Value chain is a range of related processes or activities that an industry performs to deliver products or service to the market. The example schematic below shows the value chain associated with Heineken beer production and involves crop farming; different stages of processing, production, and packaging; bulk sales/supply; retail marketing; and transportation of raw materials, waste, and finished products.

Understanding the value chain of a business helps the entrepreneur to know which segment of the business he should play in, how to differentiate himself from the competition, how to expand,

---

[6] *Stakeholder* is anyone or entity that is impacted by an activity, e.g., activity or project sponsors, personnel, suppliers, permit approvers, lenders/financiers, customers, and host community around business location or site.

consolidate, or shrink the business portfolio, where to implement cost reductions, and generate more income from value improvement activities. Understanding the value chain of a business requires some level of critical thinking.

PRODUCT VALUE CHAIN FOR BEER MANUFACTURING
("From Barley to the Bar" - Adapted from Heineken)

AGRICULTURE	PROCESSING	PRODUCTION	DISTRIBUTION	MARKETING	CONSUMER MGT
Barley production	Malt Production from Barley	Brewing & Production of Packaging Materials	Packaging, Distribution & Sales	Sales & Recycling of Packing Materials	Customer Service

RAW MATERIAL SUPPLY MANAGEMENT

MATERIALS & PRODUCT INVENTORY MANAGEMENT

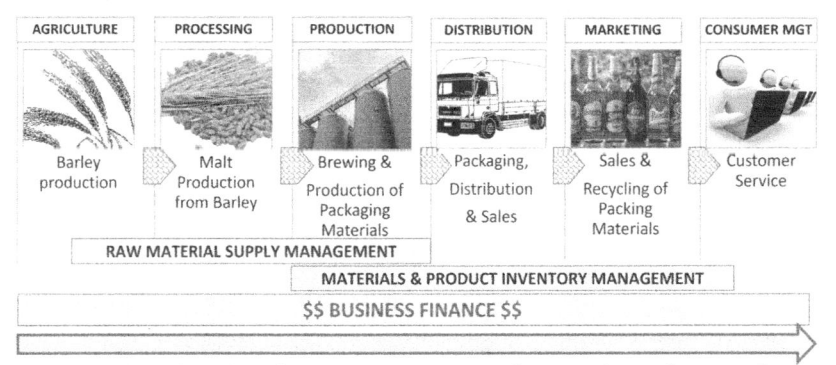

$$ BUSINESS FINANCE $$

Figure 2: Value Chain for Heineken Beer Manufacturing [Heineken, 2011]

2.4.5 Conclusion

Business acumen as a skill is not inherited but can be learned. A person can develop business acumen through combination of training and practice. From habitual practice, it becomes a way of thinking, examining issues, deciding on issues and review ongoing commitments. Closing any gap in the above skills areas will enhance a person's business performance and effectiveness.

2.5 INTERVIEWING TIPS

2.5.1 Purpose of Interviews

This section attempts to describe the basic considerations during an interview process for a vacant job and is strongly recommended for people in the job market, especially, fresh, or aspiring graduates.

The purpose of an interview is not to find out weaknesses that a candidate may have, but to see what attributes he/she can demonstrate that would match or exceed a job requirement. Where they are many candidates, the objective would then be to find out which of the candidates ranks highest in terms of knowledge, experience, business acumen and personal skills to fill a vacant job position.

Foundational knowledge in own discipline (often termed "functional skill") obtained through academic work and training are required for someone to be able to execute basic tasks on a job. As an example, a young engineer seeking a job must be able to perform basic engineering mathematical calculations and understand the concept of thermodynamics.

Equally important, every discipline has some building blocks, and the candidate must be able to demonstrate at least a basic knowledge of the building blocks in his area of expertise. Some interviewers may give a candidate a test on this during the interview. A famous example is to give a candidate a computer to quickly be able to demonstrate claimed proficiency in an IT software.

Hands-on experience is often tested with candidates being required to describe a situation where they have done a piece of work or completed some tasks. It is common to request the candidate to explain the task objectives, the methodology, key results/findings; challenges faced and how they were resolved or mitigated; and how learnings were distilled (say, through feedback or evaluation) and what improvements were implemented.

Interviewers will often interject to find out what the candidate learnt about themselves from completing challenging tasks, milestones, or projects. It will be often glaring if the candidate had no prior experience. Remember, the difference between doing something and knowing what you are doing is reflection. If you never paused to reflect on your learnings or personal developmental journey, then you would have a problem scaling through the interview process. It is often your ability to provide a good reflection on your experiences that would make interviewers believe your competency claim.

In cases where the job is for an entry position, the candidate may not be required to have much prior experience. Here, sound fundamentals in building blocks of your academic discipline are necessary and ability to quickly articulate a bigger picture (often termed "helicopter view") are then required. To be able to do well here, the candidate ought to be a person who is generally curious, and routinely engages experienced people to learn from them and improve out-of-box thinking.

Personal skill requirements depend largely on the nature of the job and the level and criticality of interfaces in the subject job position. For example, a role where the staff will work with third parties (e.g., Marketing, Contracting and Procurement, Customer Care Unit, Community Relations, etc.) requires strong communication, interface management, and negotiating skills.

2.5.2 *Interview Process and Preparations*

It is therefore very important for a candidate aspiring for a job interview to consider the following:

(a) Research the industry and company by visiting their website or social media handles – to familiarize yourself with the core business activities of the company and their business model, and then be able to infer the role(s) someone in the advertised job position might be expected to play within the organization.

(b) Clarify the reasons why you really want the job and be able to describe your selling points. Think about what you have been able to do in the past that is close to the job requirements.

(c) Anticipate possible questions from the interviewers. Sharpen your mind. You can do mock interview with someone who is experienced in a related job. This will help you tremendously in your preparation.

(d) When answering interview questions, imbibe brevity and keep your answers sharp and focused. Try not beating around the bush. The panel will easily know when you are talking nonsense or describing something you have no fair knowledge about.

(e) At the end, the interviewers may ask you if you have any questions for them. If you choose to ask questions, they must be reasonable ones. Try and formulate up to three or four sensible questions out of which you can select one or two to ask. You should not fixate on wages. Do not forget that the interview has not ended. You don't want to go off on a tangent talking nonsense. Examples of sensible questions are:

    i. What support systems does the company offer new employees?

ii. Does the company have a coaching and mentoring program to support new intakes?

iii. Would I have opportunity to handle tasks or assignments in a specific area of interest when employed?

iv. When can I expect to start work?

v. From point of offer to resumption, how much time would I have in case I need to quit a present job?

(f) Sometimes, the interviewer(s) may ask you how much you are expecting as salary. Granted that the company might have a range of what they have in mind to offer, if you are very experienced, you may be able to negotiate your proposed remuneration package. What is important is to have a sensible basis for how you arrived at your expected wage. You should have a high-level breakdown of your proposed salary. If you don't have any figure worked out, you can reply that you hope the company can offer a remuneration package that is competitive.

It does not matter if what you calculate is much higher than what they are willing to offer, you will earn some respect by showing that you have logical basis for arriving at your numbers. If you previously had a job, you could make a case for a 20-50% mark-up on your current pay package.

Overall, one very good practice is to get someone with some working administrative experience to conduct a mock interview on you, at least two weeks before the actual interview date.

2.6 MOTIVATION

2.6.1 Introduction

Motivation is an important life skill. Without motivation, one cannot achieve anything. The reason this is important is because every person on this earth is unique and has a purpose. You must be motivated to work toward your goals in order to make your dreams become a reality.

Employees with low levels of motivation typically work at a slower pace, are largely unfocused, spend more time away from their tasks, and get easily distracted by possibly occupying themselves with activities that are not value-adding. This not only results in waste of resources but also has a potential to equally affect the morale of other workers, thereby undermining the organization's ability attain the highest performance standard or meeting important targets.

2.6.2 Benefits of Motivation

People who are not motivated suffer from a myriad of poor behavioral attributes such as complacency, inertia, procrastination, low self-esteem, and loss of focus, but it is even worse when this rubs off on people around them, such as family members, associates, colleagues, and subordinates. It threatens team performance. The benefits of motivation are many:

(a) **Setting of priorities:** Once the objective is clear, motivation helps one prioritize to know what to focus on; where to invest effort, time, and money; what to avoid, or what to do less; etc.

(b) **Promotes tenacity:** Every road to success is strewn with challenges. Setbacks will make one doubt whether a goal is worth the effort, but motivation gives the courage and strength to persevere. It helps one thrive through setbacks and trials.

(c) **Weapon against fear:** Fear of failure is so common it can literally stop one from taking actions. Motivated people see beyond their fears to maintain line of sight with the anticipated outcome.

(d) **Promotes self-confidence:** When you have successfully pushed through setbacks and fear, there is a sense of accomplishment, and this builds an inner confidence to face future challenges or try something new.

(e) **Attracts like minds:** When people see that you have succeeded, they are motivated to try achieving their own dreams. If you are a motivated team leader, it will boost your team's desire to aspire toward team goals. People would also want to work with you (in a network, coaching or mentoring relationship, as partners, etc.) if they see you as highly motivated.

2.6.3 *How to Become Motivated*

Here are eight steps to achieve self-motivation:

(a) **Start simple:** Keep around your motivation triggers that remind you to get going.

(b) **Keep good company:** Make more regular encounters with positively minded and motivated people, for quick discussions and sharing of ideas. These types of people will help you grow and persevere through tough times.

(c) **Keep learning:** Research, learn and try to take in everything you can. The more you learn, the more confident you become in starting projects. Luckily, we have the internet that offers you a vast library.

(d) **Think positive:** When you encounter obstacles or challenging goals, you want to be in the habit of finding what works to get over them. Keeping your mind on the prize will help you stay strong.

(e) **Stop procrastinating:** If motivation for a particular project is low, one should get started on something else, to develop some momentum to begin the more important stuff. It is for similar reason ice breakers are run at the beginning of workshops or events, to fire people up. Once it is clear what you really need to do, it is important to really get started.

(f) **Motivation fluctuates:** The mood of an average individual fluctuates, perhaps due to personal circumstances. To prevent mood swings from derailing plans or commitments, try to identify the things that trigger bad moods or loss of interest, and avoid them. Once you are aware of these triggers, you can work around and develop the capacity to manage them. The triggers can be people, situations, environment, or perceived lack of appreciation.

(g) **Track your progress:** Track and monitor progress for ongoing activities and plan, using measurable milestones. Use feedback from stakeholders to reaffirm your strengths and weaknesses and identify areas for improvement.

(h) **Help others:** If the people you help with ideas are successful, it will help you to stay motivated knowing that you are doing something right. Be willing to share your ideas and help your associates get motivated.

2.7 STAKEHOLDER MANAGEMENT

2.7.1 Introduction

A stakeholder is anyone or group of persons that is impacted by a project or activity. Stakeholder management is the process of understanding, communicating, and developing relationships with people to facilitate smooth delivery of an activity that impacts them. Understanding their interests and needs (collectively termed "stake") enhances fit-for-purpose engagement with them and is the starting point in incorporating strategies to manage them.

If you are desiring to go to college or university, the primary stakeholders in the decision are your sponsors (who will fund your education and therefore have a say in what school can be afforded) and your family if different from sponsor. What do you think will happen if you secure admission into a private university, which your sponsor cannot not really afford?

If you want to build a family home on a parcel of land you bought from someone, your stakeholders will include landlord and neighbors (who may be affected by construction activities), workers at the site, and your own family who may have an input into the home design and functionality requirements. Town Planning Authority that approves building plans will also constitute a stakeholder as well.

2.7.2 Importance of Stakeholder Management

Key stakeholders can have a significant impact on the success of an activity or project. They may have influence and power to support or block your project from happening at all. Poor stakeholder management can lead to project slippage, cost overrun, and reputational damage.

Imagine you are a road construction contractor, and you mobilize equipment to site without first engaging the host community. You can incur hefty demurrage on hired machinery if you are stuck on site due to prolonged dispute with community stakeholders at the site.

An in-depth understanding of stakeholders combined with clear communication and engagement strategies are required to develop and maintain relationships, which are keys to smooth and hitch-free project delivery. Some of the benefits of project stakeholder management include:

(a) **Staying on deadline and within budget:** Poor management of stakeholders that have approval or endorsement rights over your activity can lead to delays, which could result in avoidable project slippage and cost overruns.

(b) **Prevents micro-managing:** Inability to manage internal stakeholders can lead to them having poor visibility of your project. This can result in apathy from valuable resources or promote micro-management of your activity by your superiors, resulting in poor line of sight.[7]

(c) **Proper utilization of stakeholder expertise:** Having an effective communication strategy with stakeholders helps you get crucial information that can enhance project delivery. This is particularly true for health, safety, environment, and security information around a project site or location. Valuable information from collaborative stakeholders, where properly managed, can lead to better project outcomes.

2.7.3 Requirements for Effective Stakeholder Management

---

[7] ***Poor line of sight*** means not being clear regarding who is in charge, or who is taking, or approving decisions.

Engagement of stakeholders is critical to meeting a project or activity delivery objectives, but they can only contribute positively if the project team engages them in a proactive manner. Thus, a proactive approach is needed to prevent potentials issues from occurring during activity execution. The following are requirements for effective stakeholder management:

(a) **Communication** is about gathering information and learning how to effectively interact with a target group. Whereas a large group can be managed through a townhall session, the leadership of a group may require a focus closed-door meeting.

(b) **Early and frequent consultations** are necessary to ensure stakeholders are properly informed about the purpose, scope, risks, and approach for a project. There is a need to communicate with them early in project life cycle to ensure requirements are understood by all parties. The reason is that inputs from stakeholders can influence the project strategy.

(c) **Maintain some level of flexibility** as humans make mistakes, so also stakeholders. Sometimes, there are personal agendas, poor attitudes, and inconsistencies in expectations or changes in demands. By understanding the root cause of a stakeholder's behavior, one can determine the best course of action to keep the relationships productive.

(d) **Prepare a stakeholder management plan** with which to engage and manage them. In projects, costs associated with delivering stakeholder management strategies should be factored into the project plans and properly funded. Plans should be fit-for-purpose and not needlessly complicated.

In very simple situations, it can be a list of stakeholders, what their interests are, purpose of engaging them, and when the engagement will take place.

(e) **Develop and maintain relationships** to create a level of trust. When people trust each other, collaboration happens more easily and yield better results. Team-building activities with stakeholders such as attending their own personal events or ceremonies can be useful for trust and relationship building. Good relationships will lead to better problem-solving and decision-making.

(f) **Prepare for uncertainties** that can be caused by the stakeholders themselves. You should have the foresight to determine possible risks and hazards that could arise from managing them. This is important to keep the project on schedule and within budget. Watch out for emergence of new stakeholders as the project matures.

(g) **Imbibe flexibility to allow for deal-making where necessary.** Stakeholders can have different opinions and ideas, which can make it difficult for an activity manager to keep everyone satisfied. It may be necessary to compromise by establishing an acceptable baseline for all involved stakeholders.

(h) **Definition of success can differ from one stakeholder to another** due to varying interests. For example, a host community to a government project may want amenities provided for them by the project contractor, such as scholarship for indigenes or employment of community members. The project would be a failure to them if these aspirations are not met. A manager should know the metrics for various stakeholders so that they can effectively manage expectations.

(i) **Ensure all stakeholders understand their responsibilities** so that they can play their parts in supporting a project activity.

2.7.4 Stakeholder Mapping

The following are steps to be taken in carrying out an effective stakeholder management process:

(a) **Be clear regarding project goals:** Before assessing stakeholders, it is important to be very clear regarding project aspirations and objectives and achieve internal alignment within the project team (if more than one person is involved in the delivery). A discordant project team engaging external stakeholders is a potential disaster in the making.

(b) **Conduct detailed stakeholder analysis:** This analysis enables one to learn about stakeholder categories and determine their characteristics (influence and interests). This stage also offers a good insight into how the stakeholder can help or hinder the project, and links to definition of responsibilities. The objectives of the analysis are as follows:

- Conduct a stakeholder workshop at the early stage of the project planning.
- Assess how identified stakeholders might be affected or might affect the project (positive/negative). You need to understand their "stakes" or interests.
- Understand what influence, authority, or powers that stakeholders can have on project plans.

- Assess how the respective stakeholders may affect or influence the project, and how best to engage or involve them.
- Assess possibility of potential conflicts amongst various stakeholders and think of how best to manage them.

Below is an example of a stakeholder group for a manufacturing activity. Stakeholders should be ranked based on their levels of influence[8] and interest[9].

Stakeholder	Influence/Interest
Project sponsor	Own the project or activity and have approval authorities over strategy, schedule, and funding.
Project team members	Carrying out project evaluations and managing the stakeholders.
Customers	Buying products; they drive revenues.
Suppliers	Bringing raw materials and other consumables critical for production
Competitors	Partly driving the market trends.
Government regulators	Agencies that approve designs and issue permits.
Shareholders	Own the business, if different from Project Sponsor.
Host community	Custodians of the location/site.

2.7.5 Stakeholder Management Strategy

A stakeholder matrix or grid (shown below) is used to help determine how much support attention that a project team needs to

---

[8] *Influence is the ability empowered by law/mandate or through social hierarchy (i.e., authority) or access to powerful actors, to shape an activity or its outcome.*

[9] *Interest is the willingness/motivation (driven by institutional mandate or civic responsibility) to be engaged in an activity.*

pay to each stakeholder. The power/interest grid divides stakeholders into four groups.

STAKEHOLDER MATRIX

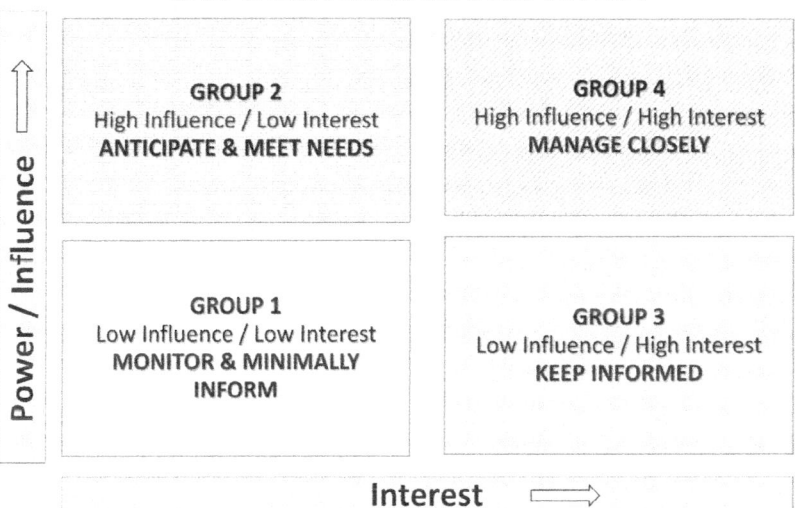

Power / Influence ↑		
	GROUP 2 High Influence / Low Interest **ANTICIPATE & MEET NEEDS**	**GROUP 4** High Influence / High Interest **MANAGE CLOSELY**
	GROUP 1 Low Influence / Low Interest **MONITOR & MINIMALLY INFORM**	**GROUP 3** Low Influence / High Interest **KEEP INFORMED**

Interest ⟹

Figure 3: Stakeholder Matrix

- **Group 1 ("Apathetics")**: This group has low influence and low interest. They should be monitored and provided only minimal communication.
- **Group 2 ("Latents")**: This group typically have high power but have low interest. They need to be provided information regarding the activity on need and strategic basis.
- **Group 3 ("Defenders")**: This group has high interest but low influence. They need to be informed about what is happening so they can identify any major concerns.
- **Group 4 ("Promoters")**: This group has high influence and high interest and should be managed carefully. Full stakeholder engagement coupled with frequent communication are needed to keep this group satisfied.

2.7.6 Creating Stakeholder Communication Plan

A communication plan makes it easier to keep stakeholders engaged effectively, keep track of when we need to communicate with them, and monitor for any potential issues that may arise from them. Once you have identified stakeholders and determined their influence and interests, you can create a communication plan, which will address:

- Their roles and expectations.
- What information need to be shared with them.
- The best method for communication with each category, frequency, and appropriate timing.
- Any funding or external resource requirement to support the engagements.

2.7.7 Conclusion

Stakeholder management is critical to the success of any activity or project. Implementing a stakeholder management plan from the beginning will help detect issues early on, foster collaboration, and keep the project on track. Managing stakeholders ultimately means forming productive relationships with them. This can turn some critical stakeholders into effective partners, which is a good thing.

Even if you do not develop a formal stakeholder management plan or follow this detailed framework, try to make it habitual to determine who your stakeholders are for any activity, their roles, and expectations, and then think through how best to manage or handle them. A key thing to remember is that stakeholder management is about effective communication and management of people who have an influence or interest in what you are doing.

2.8 SOCIAL MEDIA IN BUSINESS

2.8.1 Introduction

Social media in the modern digital age has become an effective means to stimulate conversations within the social sphere. This is an area where individuals meet, express themselves and share information. Presence of people on these sites offers potential opportunities that businesses are leveraging to market their products or services.

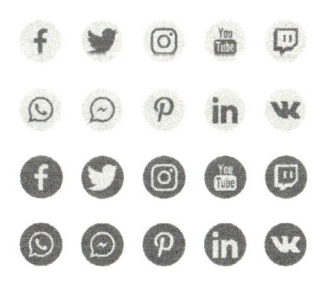

Figure 4: Social Media Platform Icons

According to Wikipedia, social media are interactive technologies that allow the creation and exchange of information, ideas, interests, and other forms of expression via virtual communities and networks.

Social platforms help connect with customers, increase awareness about your brand, and boost leads and sales. Social media was the reason why the business sector persevered during the COVID-19 lockdown in 2020/2021. If you seriously want to establish a solid presence in the market, you need to leverage where customers can be found and what they are doing. Therefore, it is about business trying to monetize social media usage by the public.

2.8.2 *Social Media Platform Types*

There are seven main categories, each with its set of characteristics. [Digital Vidya, 2022] and [Laura, 2021]:

- **Social networking sites** allow one to connect with people and entities of similar interests and backgrounds. They allow users to share thoughts, upload photos, and videos, and participate in group discussions and posts of links to news articles, whereafter users can proceed to vote on the submissions. The items with the highest number of votes are most prominently displayed. Facebook, Twitter, and Instagram are popular examples.

- **Bookmarking sites** allow users to save and organize links to any number of online resources and websites. A great feature of these sites is the ability for the users to "tag" links, which makes them easier to search, and invariably, share with their followers. Examples are Pinterest and Flipboard.

- **Social Media Sites** allow users to share different types of media such as images and videos. Many also offer social features, e.g., ability to create profiles and option of commenting on the uploaded media. These platforms mostly encourage user-generated content where anyone can create and share their creativity or spark conversations. Pinterest and YouTube are popular examples.

- **Microblogging sites** allow users to submit short-written entries, which can include links for products and services, as well as other social media sites. These are then posted on the "walls" of everyone who has subscribed to that user's account. Twitter and Facebook are examples of microblogging sites.

- **Blog comments and online forums** let users engage in conversations by posting and responding to community messages. The comments are usually centered around the specific subject of the attached blog. Google's Blogger, is a good example.
- **Social review sites** are used to share experiences from locations and services, such as holiday destinations, restaurants, and equipment purchase. When planning to buy a new car, try out a new restaurant, or book a vacation, many people first head to the reviews. Examples are TripAdvisor, FourSquare and Yelp.
- **Sharing economy networks** bring people who have got something they want to share together with those who need them, thereby giving people space to share their thoughts and express their opinions. Examples are Medium, Tumblr, Airbnb, and Pantheon.

2.8.3 *Social Media Demography and Statistics*

Internet and social medial usage are interlinked. Out of global population of internet users (web and Apps combined), about:

- 96% use internet for chats and messaging.
- 93% use it for social networks.
- 83% for search engines.
- 58% for shopping.
- 56% for maps and location services.
- Google, YouTube, Facebook, Twitter, Amazon, Instagram, and Yahoo are among the top 10 visited sites.

The popularity of a social network can be determined partly by their number of users and their frequencies of visiting the sites. These point to the potential of exposing brands to larger target audience. The following are some of the highlights of global social media usage published by Statista [2022]:

- We have an estimated 17.1bln active global social media users every month.
- The four most-used platforms are **Facebook** (~17%), **YouTube** (15%), **WhatsApp** (12%) and **Instagram** (9%). When combined, these four networks drive more than half of all social media usage.
- The other notable platforms, namely, **Snapchat**, **Telegram**, **Pinterest** and **Twitter** each contribute about 3% of the global usage.

User demographics are important in linking a social media network to your target audience. The Digital 2022 Global Overview Report [Datareportal, 2022] shows the following highlights:

- About 58% of the entire global population use social media, of which 54% are men.
- Social media usage is growing at about 10% annually.
- Out of estimated 4.2bln social media users, about 98% are active, and, in terms of age:

Age Bracket (years)	Percentage of Active Users
13-19	13%
20 – 29	32%
30 – 39	22%
40 – 49	15%
50 – 59	10%

- Over 70% of global Facebook users are within the age band of 18 to 44 (see chat below), with nearly two-third (2/3) of them being male.
- SnapChat and YouTube have the most significant proportion of younger users (18-23% of total users, with Age <18yrs), possibly because of their offer of video streams.
- About 74% of Twitter's audience is predominantly male.
- LinkedIn is predominantly used by professionals.

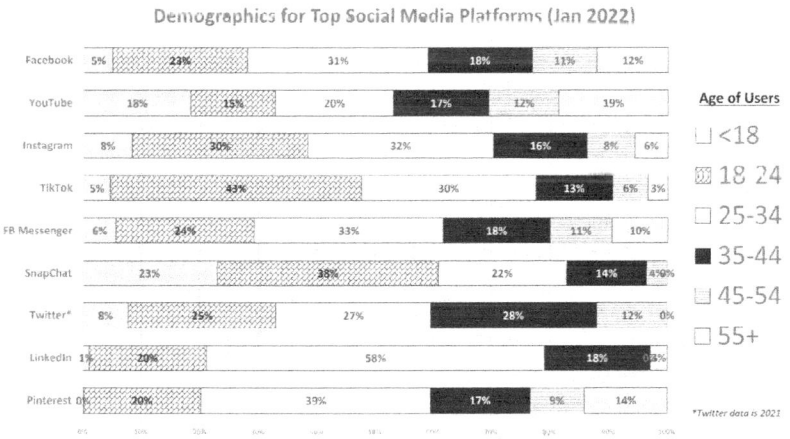

Figure 5: User Age Demographics of Popular Social Media Platforms [Datareportal, 2022]

2.8.4 Business Benefits of Social Media Usage

Social media offers a vast array of opportunities for advertising new products and services to target groups [Lyfe Marketing, 2022].

2.8.4.1 Sales Boost from Social Advertising

Unlike traditional advertising where communication is one-sided and indirect, a communicative dialogue takes place in social media. Prospective and existing customers can be reached directly, and they in turn can give feedback just as well. Social media advertising offers the following advantages:

In traditional offline advertising, the objective is to catch the interest of vast array of people out there, while with social media, one can reach out to targeted prospects. Thus, social media advertising is more reliable.

It is cheaper than traditional advertising such as print media, TV, and radio. Many social media channels can be used for free before scaling up to paid ads.

It is difficult to analyze the performance of offline advertising campaign. Paid social media ads allow you to constantly keep track of how your ad is performing. This provides opportunity to improve advertising strategy and content.

2.8.4.2 Increase Inbound Traffic

By using social media for marketing, one can diversify efforts and reach out to a versatile customer base. Outbound marketing interrupts the audience with contents they might not want, while the objective of inbound marketing is to attract customers by creating valuable social media content and experiences tailored for them. Inbound marketing is one of the effective ways to generate targeted traffic to your website, which can potentially become clients.

2.8.4.3 Increase Conversion Rates

Social media is full of activities that can be used for social proof[10]. When someone tweets about how your product changed his life, and makes a post praising your services, other people take notice and interest.

Another example is when loyal fans that follow you create content for you (termed User-Generated Content). Your followers may

---

[10] **Social proof** is a psychological phenomenon where people assume that the actions of others truly reflect correct behavior for a given situation.

mention you on a positive note, which you can then feature on your own social profile. If you have a decent audience size, you can also proactively ask people to share valuable content for a chance to get featured to a wide audience via your platform. This provides an opportunity for partnership.

2.8.4.4 Boosting Brand Awareness, Trust, and Loyalty

Social media helps increase brand value and recognition by enabling showcase of products and services. Use of eye-catching visuals in your content (e.g., images and videos) increases engagement and boosts social shares[11].

By involving the target groups in the development of new products and services, prospective buyers become active participants, sparking discussions that promote brand loyalty and at the same time generate solutions that cater to customer needs. Also, by getting target groups involved in brand discussions, companies can boost their visibility and attract more prospective buyers, some of whom might even become multipliers themselves by voluntarily advertising the products or services.

2.8.4.5 Improve Search Engine Optimization

Today, a search is not limited to the traditional web search engines. People are no longer dependent on Google search when they need to connect to something or someone. Social media platforms such as Facebook and Twitter that generate and share massive amounts of content, offer robust search engines as well.

---

[11] ***Social sharing*** *describes when social media users broadcast web content on a social network to their connections, groups, or specific individuals. One of the primary aims of corporate social media marketing is to generate brand awareness by leveraging existing audience to share content.*

Content can easily be discovered by users with the help of keyword search, hashtags, etc. When people search for the type of content published on your social media page, you may win new fans that want to follow, connect, and do business with you. When people see great content being created and shared, they will become curious and would want to look it up to learn more.

2.8.4.6 Customer Care Management

Social media offers a communication channel for customer service and support. Customers can send product and support queries or feedback in just a few clicks and without the usual red tape associated with calling Customer Care Center, and companies can then respond just as conveniently and easily. Responding to customer inquiries publicly, not being afraid of criticism, and confidently solving a problem promotes transparency and demonstrates service quality.

2.8.4.7 Access to Skilled Professionals

Social networking sites are indispensable to employer branding and perfectly suited to building an appealing employer image. Job postings can also be uploaded and shared there by users. Traditional advertisers are losing out rapidly against social media in terms of job placements.

2.8.5 Factors Influencing Choice of Media Platform for Business

There are many social media platforms out there, and one must carefully select a few that will really benefit his business. The following are key considerations when deciding which platform(s) to use.

(a) Number of users: The popularity of a social network can be determined partly by their number of users and their frequency of visiting the sites. These point to the potential of exposing your brand to a larger audience.

(b) User demographics: You would want the demographics of a social media network to be aligned to your target audience. For example, if you sell fashion wears and accessories, your target audience would be young people and mid-career individuals. Facebook has a large youthful followership. Conversely, a social network such as LinkedIn, aimed at professionals, would be most suitable for marketing of office software solutions.

(c) Type of content being shared: The type of content for your target audience needs to be aligned with the contents a specific platform is optimized for.

Twitter is mostly about posting a short amount of text, whereas Instagram is more about images. Thus, if you sell home décor goods requiring display of goods, then Instagram is a great choice.

If you are planning on writing short pieces of content that are casual in tone, then Facebook is a good place. However, if you are planning on writing more in-depth articles, LinkedIn would be a better choice.

Facebook accepts almost any type of content, from simple status update to a long- article. In contrast, defined character limit in Twitter makes it necessary to be very concise and straight to the point.

(d) Frequency of updates/posts: Contents are not just articles and blogs; they also refer to the updates that you make. Therefore, you need to consider how often you plan on posting contents and whether you are going to be able to cope with daily posts. A Twitter presence requires multiple daily posts to keep up with your users, whereas you can get away with two or three quality posts per week on LinkedIn or Facebook.

Additionally, consider whether the content on social channels complement each other. For example, most companies will use Twitter hashtags on their Instagram page and also post YouTube videos on their Facebook page.

(e) Paid advertising options: Promotional content on social media is a cheap way to advertise, but you may not wish to depend solely on your followers' decision to share or like your content. Sometimes, you want to explore social media sites that offer paid advertising options allowing the targeting of content to specific audience. LinkedIn, Facebook, and Twitter are good examples.

(f) Analytics: Most social media sites provide built-in functionality to assess followership and site activity. Based on the assessment, one can optimize the marketing strategy to make it more effective.

For example, Facebook Insights provides a free analytics tool that can be used to understand demographics of the audience, how many people are discovering, and how many are responding to posts.

Some analytics tools are more in-depth while others are simpler and user-friendly. The type of tools you should look for depends on your skill level. There are also some social media platforms that are supported by third party analytics tools.

(g) Additional Functionalities: Image optimization is a good example of valuable functionality that enhances social media campaign. Image uploading is present in all social media platforms, but some allow some type of image processing. Facebook for example allows the creation of photo albums, while Instagram boasts of several different filters to enhance photos prior to upload and is perfect for showcasing products.

2.8.6 *Creating a Social Media Plan for Business*

Without a strategy, one might be posting on social media platforms for the sake of posting something out there. Without understanding the objectives, who your target audience is, and what they want, it would be hard to achieve the desired results. For those that want to work as social media consultants, developing a marketing strategy is equally essential [SproutSocial, 2022]. Below are the key steps.

2.8.6.1 Defining Social Media Goals

The first step is to articulate the objectives you want to achieve. Ask yourself the following questions:

- What is my goal for creating social media pages?
- Who is my target audience, and what are the best ways to reach out to them?
- Would I like to pay for adverts on the platform?

2.8.6.2 Selection of Social Media Platform

Selection criteria include social media objectives, types of content supported by sites, user demographics, and availability of paid advertisement functionality and tools for analyzing followership and user activity. For example, Instagram will feature pictures and videos, Twitter requires brief texts of no more than 150 characters, while Snapchat works well with videos. In places where internet data is not cheap, use of videos should be minimized.

2.8.6.3 Content Creation and Resourcing

You need to focus on your target audience to create leads and must have a way of measuring the level of achievement attained. For example, you can look at the target number of new followers achieved by a certain timeline.

In terms of resourcing, you need to have a person skilled in handling social media tasks, including content development and keeping your site active. In developing countries with low IT literacy and penetration within the general population, businesses are resorting to hiring social media consultants. This same resource can additionally provide customer care support and handle product inquiries.

Social media consultancy is offering significant job opportunities for young graduates in developing countries. I know one of my proteges who is working (remotely) as a social media handler for three separate companies.

2.8.6.4 Interaction with Audience to Understand their Needs

Responses to posts and comments encourages the audience to follow you. When interacting with your audience, understand their needs, try to figure out what they want to read about and create engaging posts and comments. Discussion about some aspects of your business will portray you as an expert and an interesting person they can follow.

2.8.6.5 Share Your Social Media Accounts

Make people around you are probably aware of your business presence on popular social media networks. When making a post on a social media platform, add a link to your email and website to generate more leads. Also, have social media icons for visitors to your website to follow your social media pages.

2.8.6.6 Use Keywords and Hashtags on Social Media Accounts

When using keywords for social media, focus on using keywords related to your business. Use words that are commonly searched for on Google. Also, using trending hashtags related to your business will attract more users to your platform.

2.8.6.7 Entice Audience with Games and Gifts

Make your posts engaging to draw more attention, likes, and followers, by developing quality content, including questions and games, where possible. You can also use the reward system by offering discounts for products and free trials, to entice your audience and earn more followership.

2.8.6.8 Maintain Regular Pace of Content Posting

Your audience will always look forward to your posts if they are captivating and engaging. Posting regularly at consistent intervals will give your audience content to look forward to and the customers reason to connect with you on your social media handles. You can publish your posts at regular intervals, such as once or twice daily, five times weekly and so on. You can schedule your posts using automation tools to save more time and make your postings appear regularly.

2.8.6.9 Use of Frequently Asked Questions (FAQs)

FAQs help your audience, clients or customers resolve service issues or complaints. You can highlight FAQs relating to complaints you have resolved in the past or use questions likely to be asked by your audience. Your audience will always spend more time on your social media page when you use FAQs to help them answer questions about your service provision.

2.8.6.10 Planning and Content Optimization

If you already have an idea that is working well in getting you more followers and generating new leads, stick with it. Strategizing, planning, and keeping in tune with the evolving social media trends will help you gather and retain more followers on the social media network.

Social media platforms are quite different, which is why you need to optimize your posts to meet each platform requirement. Use appropriate posts and contents on each social media platform to share the same message. Use pictures and videos for Instagram, brief texts for Twitter, and videos for Snapchat.

2.8.7 Conclusions

Social media is one of the fastest growing means of communication and information sharing. If you want to grow personally and grow your business as well, you really need to leverage the social media train. To make this work, you need to have a sound strategy and resourcing plan.

Entrepreneurs who are not social media savvy or might not have time to regularly generate and update media content should employ social media handlers. Such persons can also play a dual role in the organization, or can be employed on part-time and remote basis, thereby making their services more affordable.

For those that want to learn more about specific social media marketing tools, there are increasing number of sites offering online training services. Udemy [2022] offers affordable variety of online marketing courses, with many tailored to specific social media platforms, including Instagram, Facebook, TikTok, LinkedIn and Social Media Market and Social Media management in general.

REFERENCES

1. Wikipedia. (2022). *Truthiness*. Retrieved Mar 23, 2022, from https://en.wikipedia.org/wiki/Truthiness
2. Wikipedia. (2022). *Pareto Principle*. Retrieved Mar 23, 2022, from https://en.wikipedia.org/wiki/Pareto_principle
3. Wikipedia. (2022). *Parkinson's Law*. Retrieved Mar 23, 2022, from https://en.wikipedia.org/wiki/Parkinson%27s_law.
4. Heineken (2011). *Heineken's Supply Chain*. Retrieved from http://www.sustainabilityreport.heineken.com/2011/overview/brewing-a-better-future.html.
5. Digital Vidya, Gurgaon (2022, Feb). *What are the Different Types of Social Media?* Retrieved Jan 18, 2022, from https://www.digitalvidya.com/blog/types-of-social-media/
6. Laura Wong (2021, Sep). *Nine (9) Types of Social Media and How Each Can Benefit Your Business*. Retrieved Jan 18, 2022, from https://blog.hootsuite.com/types-of-social-media/
7. Statista. (2022). *Popular Social Networks Worldwide as of January 2022, Ranked by Number of Monthly Active Users*. Retrieved Mar 23, 2022, from https://www.statista.com/statistics/272014/global-social-networks-ranked-by-number-of-users/.
8. Datareportal. (2022). Digital 2022 Global Overview Report, Retrieved Mar 30, 2022, from https://datareportal.com/reports/?tag=Global+Overview.
9. Lyfe Marketing. (2022). *The Importance of Social Media in Business*. Retrieved Mar 23, 2022, from https://www.lyfemarketing.com/blog/importance-social-media-business/

10 SproutSocial. (2022). *Social Media Marketing Strategy.* Retrieved Mar 23, 2022, from https://sproutsocial.com/insights/social-media-marketing-strategy/

11 Udemy. (2022). *Social Media Marketing Courses.* Retrieved Mar 23, 2022, from https://www.udemy.com/courses/marketing/social-media-marketing/